THE
COURAGE
OF
MAGIC JOHNSON

THE COURAGE OF MAGIC JOHNSON

*From
Boyhood Dreams
to Superstar
to His Toughest
Challenge*

PETER F. PASCARELLI

BANTAM BOOKS
NEW YORK • TORONTO • LONDON • SYDNEY • AUCKLAND

THE COURAGE OF MAGIC JOHNSON
A Bantam Book / January 1992

ISBN 0-553-29915-8

Published simultaneously in the United States and Canada

Bantam Books are published by Bantam Books, a division of
Bantam Doubleday Dell Publishing Group, Inc. Its trademark,
consisting of the words "Bantam Books" and the portrayal of a
rooster, is Registered in U.S. Patent and Trademark Office and in
other countries. Marca Registrada. Bantam Books, 666 Fifth
Avenue, New York, New York 10103.

PRINTED IN THE UNITED STATES OF AMERICA

RAD   0 9 8 7 6 5 4 3 2 1

J
B

Thanks to Beverly Horowitz, Lauren Field, and all the people at Bantam for working so hard to get this project done. Thanks also to Stan Drate, Folio Graphics Company, Inc., and Wide World Photos.

As always nothing could be accomplished without the home team—Betsy, Paige, Patrick, David, Robyn, Greg, and Elizabeth.

Finally, a hope and prayer that Magic Johnson can be the key to unlocking the mystery of the AIDS virus and that he and all sufferers can beat this terrible disease.

Contents

1

Magic's Shocking News

On November 7, 1991, a smoggy Thursday afternoon, Magic Johnson announced at a Los Angeles press conference that he was retiring as a professional basketball player after testing positive for the HIV virus, which causes AIDS. He later stated that he had acquired the virus through numerous female partners and a failure to practice safe sex.

The announcement created a thunderclap that was unprecedented in the history of American sports, speaking volumes about Magic's fame and popularity. For the first time ever, all major television networks—ABC, CBS, NBC, and

CNN—led their nightly newscasts with a sports story. Every daily newspaper in the country and many others around the world had Magic Johnson on the front page the next morning. At a press conference in Rome where he was attending a meeting of NATO leaders, the first question asked of President Bush concerned Magic Johnson.

Some commentators suggested that only the assassination of President John F. Kennedy had more shock value than Johnson's revelation, that people would remember where they were when they heard Johnson had tested HIV positive just as they remembered where they were in 1963 when they heard that JFK had been shot in Dallas.

In New York's Madison Square Garden, some of the most cynical fans in the world stood with tears in their eyes as they were led in the Lord's Prayer by players and Knicks coach Pat Riley, who with Johnson created the Lakers' magical "Showtime" style of play.

In Charlotte, North Carolina, young Hornets guard Rex Chapman announced he and his wife were donating $50,000 to AIDS research.

Fans in NBA arenas wept as they offered silent prayers for Johnson.

And in cities all over the country, AIDS hotlines reported that their phones were jammed with an unheard-of number of calls from people suddenly made aware of the HIV virus and inquiring about testing procedures.

Why this overwhelming reaction?

For one thing, this was not just another athlete. Few sports figures of his generation were more popular than Magic Johnson. With a smile on his face and an unquenchable zest for the game, Johnson engraved himself on the nation's consciousness. Long before Michael Jordan leaped into America's living rooms, Johnson had been the main reason that basketball became the sport of the 1990s. He was the ultimate team player and winner, a champion at every level at which he played.

His style of play set him apart from all who had come before him. Johnson's trademark was a breathtaking, high-speed display of creativity. His ultimate goal seemed to be not scoring but involving as many teammates as possible. His sleight-of-hand passing and ball-handling were made all the more remarkable by his size: six feet, nine inches. All the while, he laid his emotions out for all to see, angrily scolding a teammate for playing too much to the crowd, anguishing when one of his swooping drives to the basket didn't pay dividends, or melting hearts with the biggest smile in the world when the Lakers won another game.

Magic Johnson had transcended being solely an exciting basketball player. He was also a man of towering personal integrity who annually staged a successful exhibition game that brought together the NBA's biggest stars for the benefit of the United Negro College Fund. He gave his time unfailingly to other charities, for which he helped raise several million dollars a year. And his impeccable public image made him a highly desired public spokesman for corporations such as Pepsi, Converse, and Nintendo. His bulging portfolio promised a future as a major player in the world of business when his career on the basketball court ended.

The sheer enormous fact of Magic Johnson's testing positive for the HIV virus was almost impossible to comprehend. AIDS was a disease which most people associated only with homosexuals and drug users, not with a young sports superstar and dashing ladies' man whose friends included some of the biggest names in Hollywood. Superstars weren't supposed to get AIDS, least of all anyone as popular as Magic. He was that rarest of public figures—liked, even loved, by fans in every city, not just in Los Angeles, where he was as big as the biggest of the entertainment world's stars. In a time when grandiose salaries and arrogant attitudes had alienated so many fans from their sports heroes, Magic was a remarkable exception. He had become a modern symbol of what a sports hero should be—unselfish, a humble yet exuberant winner who played the game with flair and a pure joy rarely seen before, hugely successful in the business world, a model for young black men, a tireless contributor to the community.

All over the sports world, drug scandals and endless contract talk, altercations with fans, and personal surliness had robbed sports of much of their innocence and reinforced the sad truth that this was a cold business like every other. But Magic Johnson was the exception, and now he faced being struck down by a disease that most Americans felt was reserved for a particular segment of society, not for one of the marquee names of the sports world. The shock was mind-numbing. Just as numbing was the fear. If Magic Johnson could have the HIV virus, so could anyone. The disease people didn't like to talk about had suddenly been brought home to everyone.

But besides the tragic news, there was something else remarkable about that November press conference. The way Johnson handled the news left nearly as powerful an impression on the nation as the announcement itself. How he dealt with this new and potentially deadly chapter in his public life defined the measure of the man.

Magic's career has been full of magnificent performances—the besting of Larry Bird to win the 1979 NCAA title, the day in Philadelphia when as a rookie he played center, forward, and guard in leading the Lakers to the NBA title, all those amazing nights when he made the term "triple-double" (double figures in points, rebounds, and assists) his personal property, the five World Championships of which he was a part, the MVP performances in the regular season, playoffs, and All-Star games. However, no Johnson masterpiece could top his performance that Thursday afternoon before a packed conference room and national TV cameras in the Great Western Forum, which had been his personal stage for a dozen years.

Some commentators complained weeks later that Johnson somehow managed his publicity and that while the world should obviously be sympathetic, he should not become a hero. However, at that press conference and in the days following, Magic never tried to hide the way he had likely contracted the virus, nor did he ever try to pretend that he was a hero for admitting he had it. From the beginning of his ordeal, Johnson made it clear he was well aware of the implications and the cruel realities.

By his side that afternoon was his wife, Cookie, his college sweetheart, to whom he had been married less than two months and who was just weeks pregnant. Johnson spoke of his initial horror that perhaps he had infected her and the baby, but Cookie tested negative for the HIV virus. Johnson later acknowledged concern for other women with whom he had had sex before his marriage, whom he could have infected.

Johnson revealed that before the press conference he had called his ten-year-old son, Andre, who was born out of wedlock and lives in Michigan with his mother. Johnson has been a loving father to his child, and on that darkest of days he wanted to reassure the youngster that no matter what he heard, his father was fine and was thinking of him.

Flanking Johnson in the Forum were Lakers owner Dr. Jerry Buss and general manager Jerry West, whose decision to give Johnson a $3 million loan had led to the insurance company's physical exam that first revealed Johnson had the HIV virus. These men now had lost their franchise's greatest player, whose absence would have an inestimable impact upon the Lakers' future fortunes. But they stood with Johnson on that bleak day, as did former teammates like Kareem Abdul-Jabbar and NBA commissioner David Stern, who better than anyone else knew that Johnson had been a prime force in rescuing the NBA from financial misery and a second-rate image, in the process elevating the league to a new plateau of worldwide prosperity and popularity.

Johnson exhibited honesty beyond the norm of most public figures by frankly acknowledging he had acquired the virus and confronting the grim implications. That any public figure, much less one of Johnson's almost mythic stature, would make such a declaration had seemed unthinkable. But Johnson stood tall in a dark suit, without tears and occasionally flashing the smile for which he was world-famous. With remarkable good humor and determination, he seemed to be trying to reassure all those listening who were so wounded by the shock of his announcement. "I'm still going to be around," he said. "I'm going to beat it and I'm going to have fun."

Johnson vowed to preach the message of safe

sex. He promised to work to help the public understand and prevent the spread of AIDS, later volunteering to become a member of the President's AIDS task force. Though his dignified and upbeat message left close friends, fans who had never met him, and hard-bitten reporters weeping openly, Johnson walked away from his press conference with his head held high, on a mission to confront what he called "another challenge, another chapter in my life."

In one remarkable defining moment, he had become a symbol of a disease that had already infected more than 1 million and killed close to 150,000 and now seemed to be intruding upon the mainstream of society. In that one moment, he had come to define an entire generation which had often lived fast and loose and had now seen the tragic price such behavior could demand.

The life of Magic Johnson is no more important than any of the lives of the millions of others infected by the HIV virus. Nor should the casual sex that apparently led to his being infected be condoned. But the life of Magic Johnson can inspire others to practice the values of courage, integrity, hard work, and dignity he exhibited that awful day in November.

The world was saddened by having to say good-bye to Magic Johnson, the basketball player. But in the process, we were introduced to Earvin Johnson, Jr., a man of towering courage and integrity who would go on to use his own tragedy to touch millions more lives than could ever be reached from the basketball court.

2

Earvin Johnson, Jr., Becomes "Magic"

He was only a skinny high school sophomore. Born August 14, 1959 in Lansing, Michigan, Earvin Johnson had basketball skills far beyond his age and had already begun developing a flair for the game that set him apart from other precocious high school stars. He was getting attention beyond his immediate neighborhood. He was already being talked about as a star of the future, someone destined for the high-profile world of big-time college athletics and maybe, someday, the National Basketball Association.

It was 1974 in Lansing, Michigan, and on a particular Friday afternoon, Earvin Johnson led his Everett High School team to an easy victory in which he scored 36 points, grabbed 18 rebounds, handed out 16 assists, and made 20 steals. Reporting the game for the *Lansing State Journal* was Fred Stabley, Jr., today a college sports information director. Stabley could hardly believe the incredible performance he had just seen. He realized that he had just witnessed not only a special game but a special individual. And Stabley decided that this special player needed a nickname that would set him apart from others, that would capture the extraordinary talents this amazing kid exhibited.

Stabley's first idea was "The Big E," for Earvin. But former University of Houston and NBA star Elvin Hayes already had taken that nickname and made it well known in the sports world. So Stabley kept thinking, kept recalling the wondrous game he had just watched. The word that kept coming to mind as he thought of Johnson's play was "magic." To see a kid so young, so big, and so able to handle and pass the ball with such amazing skill, to play so unselfishly though he was obviously so much more talented than most of the other players on the court—and to do it with so much enthusiasm, so much innocence, and so little arrogance—was indeed "magic." So Stabley finally said to Earvin, "Let's call you Magic." That sounded all right to Johnson. A legend was born.

Years later, Johnson's Laker teammates called him "Buck." His family and closest friends, like

Lakers coach Pat Riley, still called him "Earvin" or "Junior." But from that time on, the world called him "Magic." It would become one of the few names or nicknames that brought instant identification. Hear the name "Michael" nowadays and you know it means Michael Jordan. Hear "Bo" and you know it's Bo Jackson. A few years ago, you didn't have to say anything more in baseball than "Reggie." And virtually no one in America says "Who?" when the name "Magic" is mentioned.

Johnson would come to be defined by the nickname. Still, his style of play and approach to the game, and to life, were not all tricks or flash or sleight of hand. Indeed, many years later Coach Riley would sometimes almost lament the nickname. As he once said, "Earvin is in a lot of ways an old-fashioned player in that he is so funda mentally sound in all aspects. Calling him Magic somehow suggests he's doing it with tricks instead of hard work and fundamentals and knowledge of the game."

Indeed, Earvin Johnson growing up was nurtured by timeless American virtues like hard work, family love, and discipline which served him well throughout his life. There was nothing magical about Johnson's upbringing or about how he became the man he became. He was one of ten children who grew up in a working-class Lansing neighborhood, raised by loving and demanding parents and put on a path to success largely paved with the values drilled into him by his father, Earvin, Sr.

The older Johnson held down two full-time jobs to support his family. He worked a 5-P.M.-to-1-A.M. shift on an automobile assembly line at a nearby General Motors plant, and he had his own hauling service, picking up trash and performing other tasks. Johnson often talked of how his father would sometimes return from his shift at the auto plant, go out again to scrub down the oil-covered floor of a local garage, return home for a few hours' sleep, wake up and finish his hauling jobs, and then take a brief nap before returning to the auto plant. Working hard was part of life. And even when Earvin, Jr., had acquired the nickname "Magic," he knew he had to get up early to help his father work on the hauling truck, or perhaps shovel ice from a neighbor's front steps, or run errands for his mother, or help with his brothers and sisters.

But there also was time for basketball. Earvin, Sr., when he had spare moments, began teaching his son the game he loved. Johnson was in grade school when his father began taking him out on the driveway and instructing him in the proper way to shoot lay-ups or dribble or pass. From an early age, even when Johnson had difficulty reaching the rim with a shot, Earvin, Sr., taught the importance of learning to handle the ball equally well with both hands. Father and son would sit together and watch NBA games, with Earvin, Sr., pointing out fundamentals and the game's finer points. Earvin, Sr., drilled into Junior the importance of developing all aspects of his game—shooting, passing, dribbling with both hands, rebounding and defense, court sense. Maybe most importantly, father taught son that the game should be played in a certain way: This was a team game and beyond that, a player must learn the fundamentals of all the game's facets; he can't call himself a player if he practices only one thing.

Many years later, Magic looked back on those sessions and realized he would never have been the player he had become without his father. "I know I was very fortunate to have been coached at an early age by the best teacher in the world—my father," he wrote in his book *Magic's Touch.* "He's the reason I'm playing the way I am now. When I received my second MVP Award in 1989, I thought of him, just as I did in 1987 when I won the award for the first time. He and my mom, who taught me the value of maintaining a down-to-earth perspective on my life, were definitely Most Valuable Parents."

Earvin, Jr., quickly fell in love with basketball. From the start, he never minded spending hours working on his game. Throughout his career, he seemed to love practicing just as much as playing. Coaches always try to drum into their players that they should practice the way they play. Johnson was always a model of the hardworking approach. When he had become the game's biggest star, he often showed up for practice an hour or two early to work on particular facets of his game. One of the first things he installed in his palatial Los Angeles home was a full-size basketball court. He simply loved to play basketball, whether it was friendly one-on-one games with friends, or shooting 500 practice jump shots alone, or playing a playoff game in front of 18,000 screaming fans and a national television audience.

In the off-season, instead of resting from the rigors of the long NBA season, Johnson often worked overtime to improve his game. After the 1986 season, Lakers coach Pat Riley urged Johnson to work on his shooting; Riley believed the Lakers needed Johnson to score more points in the coming seasons. Kareem Abdul-Jabbar was getting on in years and Johnson had to assume more of the scoring load. So Johnson worked overtime—on his own court, in charity games, and in summer leagues. He added four points a game to his scoring average and captured another Most Valuable Player award. In high school, no one had practiced harder than Johnson. And years later, his Laker teammates would often say, "Magic plays harder in practices than he does in games."

Johnson stressed such work habits in the many summer camps for youths he operated over the years. He preached how important hard work and discipline were to achieving success, the same sermons that Earvin, Sr., had repeated to him. He greeted his campers with a promise that they would work hard, that he would push them beyond whatever limits they might have thought they had. Some of his pupils began to think that Johnson wasn't the nice guy everyone thought he was. But by the end of those camps, most youngsters hated to leave and came away with valuable lessons taught by Magic.

Johnson recalled in *Magic's Touch* that when he was sent on an errand by his mother, he would always take along his basketball. He would dribble with one hand for one block and switch hands for the next. He would make a game out of trying to miss the cracks in the sidewalk. He would shoot on the local playground until it was too dark to see. He would play against local players years older than himself and hold his own. By the time he was in the fourth grade, he was playing in four different leagues. He became an accomplished ball-handler at a very early age, learning behind-the-back and between-the-legs moves years before his contemporaries tried such maneuvers.

Throughout his career, he was known more for his passing than any other aspect of his game; this had begun in elementry school. He was also deservedly acclaimed for being the ultimate team player, unselfish in his approach and always looking for ways to involve teammates in the scoring.

Inches taller than any other player and possessing far superior dribbling skills, Johnson dominated games. He could score every point his team scored without ever giving up the ball. His teammates didn't necessarily mind because they could stand back and watch Johnson win every game, but the kids' parents became angry that no one scored except Magic. At some games, some parents began yelling at Johnson to pass the ball and allow their child to shoot. They would yell at the coach to "get the Johnson kid out so our kids can have a chance." The bad feeling put pressure on Johnson, who was only about ten years old, an age when such problems shouldn't have existed. The dilemma was real. Johnson learned to swallow hard and change the way he played. He would involve his teammates and make a team effort.

Johnson's decision would change his game style. In the process, he kept the peace. He involved his teammates by passing the basketball and giving other kids the chance to shoot. At the same time, Johnson didn't have to sacrifice winning, because if his teammates missed, he almost always got the rebound and put it back in the basket. Everyone was well served. Johnson's teammates and their parents felt part of the action. The team still won every game. And Johnson had taught himself some very important lessons. He learned that he could make his teammates better without giving up his own enjoyment of the game or the performance of his team. He learned that playing a team game made winning more enjoyable, that it was the proper way to play. He learned that he could do the right thing when faced with pressure.

That would be the way Johnson approached basketball and life. Winning and unselfishness would become his trademarks. Johnson quickly became a high school basketball legend in Michigan, playing for an Everett High School team that in his senior year won a state championship.

Johnson was fortunate to be coached by George Fox, a man who emphasized discipline, defense, and team play. Though Magic was the team's star and perhaps the best high school player in America, he was treated like just another member of the team. Fox would have his players repeat drill after drill after drill. If a player didn't practice hard, he didn't play in the games. That rule included Magic, who during his sophomore year, when he acquired his nickname, began loafing a bit in practice and not taking Coach Fox's drills seriously enough. Finally, Fox brought Johnson into his office and said if Johnson didn't play hard in practice, he wouldn't start in the next game. Johnson got the message.

"The players wanted to play hard for Coach Fox because he recognized and cared for us as individuals, just like any father would," wrote Johnson in *Magic's Touch*. "He was a guy we could talk to when we needed someone to listen. Having that kind of coach, someone who's more than a coach, is very important for young players."

In high school, Johnson would often score no more than a dozen or so points, but he would add something like 18 assists and 15 rebounds. However, when he opened his senior season, he changed for a time. He was under intense scrutiny by the media and fans because he had become a high school All-American. There was speculation about whether he would stay home and play his college ball at Michigan State or accept a scholarship from one of the hundreds of other interested schools. Like so many other talented kids of his age, Johnson fell victim to self-centeredness that can come from that kind of attention. He began playing as if he could win games single-handedly, going on a scoring binge that saw him average close to 40 points for the first few weeks of the season. Coach Fox quickly brought him back to earth by reminding him that basketball was a team game, not just Magic's game. Fox said if Johnson continued to play selfishly, he'd cost his team the chance of winning a state championship.

Again Johnson got the message. He returned to the unselfish style that involved all his teammates and in the process, created a better team whose every player felt part of its success. The team sometimes averaged 40-point victories on the way to winning the state championship.

But while the kid they now called Magic was getting statewide acclaim and attention from the nation's colleges, Earvin, Sr., made sure that Junior kept his growing fame in perspective.

Magic recalled being awakened on Saturday mornings by his father, who would ask how the team had played the previous night. Earvin, Sr., often was unable to see his son play because he was working. Magic would mumble in his sleep that (as usual), they had won. Whereupon the father would say, "Great, now get up because you still have to work on the truck." Earvin, Jr., was still required to do chores, even if he was among the most famous high school athletes in the country. And though Johnson never lost sight of how special a player he was, he was never allowed to become spoiled or acquire a superstar mentality.

By the end of high school, there was no more highly regarded high school player in the country than Magic Johnson. Coaches drooled over his flair and his ability, even at that early age, to make the team around him better. "We thought he would come in and be able to contribute right away," said coach Jud Heathcote of Michigan State. "But the more we saw of him, we realized he would be a dominant player whose enthusiasm would be contagious to the rest of the team." Indeed, there was no prolonged recruiting battle for Johnson's skills. He made up his mind that he would stay at home and attend Michigan State in East Lansing.

One reason was that even with all his success, Magic had modest goals. The discipline he had learned at home helped him keep his ambitions in perspective. Johnson often said that upon entering Michigan State, he would be happy just to play some college basketball, earn a degree, and be able to get a job after graduating in order to earn enough money for an apartment and a car. Such modesty would help Johnson better appreciate those around him and help him relate to his teammates, who might not be as talented but who had their own ambitions and wanted to contribute in some way to the team.

Magic, of course, would go far beyond those early modest goals, beginning at Michigan State, where his legend soon expanded outside Michigan's borders and into the national consciousness. But his character had already been well developed. The values he learned by working hard beside his father, passing the ball in fourth-grade games, and practicing hard at Everett High School would still be his foundation even when he was one of the biggest stars in the world.

As George Fox said years later on the day when Magic revealed he had contracted the HIV virus, "He was a dream come true, a product of Lansing, just a beautiful person who bettered everyone that came in contact with him."

Epic Games Define Magic

Larry Bird and Magic Johnson have been united by basketball. Throughout their careers, they were bitter rivals, but later they became close friends. Despite Magic's retirement, he still hopes he can play in the 1992 Olympics. If so, Magic and Bird will continue their unique relationship and might even be teammates.

Whatever happens in the future, their history remains well documented. Their emergence as the game's two biggest stars is largely credited with triggering the basketball boom of the 1980s that continues today unchecked. Their efforts combined to help rescue the NBA and propel it to the heights it now enjoys. The renaissance began in 1979 when Bird and Johnson were still college players. Bird brought his Indiana State team and Johnson his Michigan State team to Salt Lake City for the NCAA title game that became the most-watched college basketball game of all time.

It was a fascinating matchup. College basketball had never seen two more interesting performers than Johnson and Bird. Magic was a revolutionary player, a six-foot, 9-inch point guard in a position which had always been reserved for much smaller men. Magic controlled games with great passing and skill, all the while glowing with a smile that no one could resist. Bird, meanwhile, had old-timers similarily searching for comparisons. No one could remember a forward with a better pure outside shot, a better-developed court sense, or better passing skills. And no one had seen a forward orchestrate an entire team the way Bird could do it with his uncanny passing ability and knowledge of the game.

Meanwhile, the two programs in which Johnson and Bird played were very different. Johnson had entered a Michigan State program that played in the rough and tough Big Ten Conference, where three teams tied for first place in 1979. While Johnson was obviously the star of the team and the catalyst for everything the Spartans did, Magic had also joined a team that was loaded with talent. It included tough inside scorer Greg Kelser, a future high draft choice whose injuries killed his chances for NBA success. There was Jay Vincent, a good-shooting forward and another high draft choice who played several years in the NBA and whose brother, Sam Vincent, also played pro basketball. The other two starters, Don Bergovich and Terry Donnally, though not of pro caliber, were excellent outside shooters. It was a perfect team for Magic to orchestrate. He had a wealth of offensive weapons to distribute the ball.

No defense could key on Magic because he had so many ways to choose. And he could always reserve for himself the option of shooting. Though his shot looked unorthodox (he never had a classic shooting style), he constantly improved as an outside shooter. His size, power, and touch made him almost impossible to stop when he decided to power the ball inside himself. On top of all that, the Spartans were coached by hard-nosed Jud Heathcote, a strict disciplinarian who preached a tough defense that was the strongest part of this Michigan State team's game. As Johnson said years later, "Everyone talked about Magic Johnson versus Larry Bird being the key to that championship game but it was more about who played better defense."

Bird was almost the whole show on the Indiana State team, which had captured the nation's attention by winning its way into the championship game with a 33–0 record. Indiana State did not play as rugged competition as Michigan

State did in the Big Ten. Indiana's overall talent was not close to Michigan State's. Yet Indiana won its way through the NCAA tournament. Bird was a superb player surrounded by a lot of hard-working, but average, players. It was a measure of his greatness that he elevated his team to the highest level of college basketball. He carried Indiana State as few individuals have ever carried a team, punctuating the effort with a magnificent performance against DePaul in the semifinal game, in which at one point he hit ten straight shots to lead Indiana State into its epic meeting with Magic and Michigan State. Johnson said years later, "I had never seen Larry play until we watched him in that game against De-Paul. And I had never seen anyone like him. He wouldn't let his team lose. He made every shot, he made every pass. It was something to watch."

Heathcote has always been known for the way he prepares his teams. They have not always had the talent to beat Big Ten powers like Indiana or Michigan, but they are never beaten because of lack of preparation. Heathcote drilled his teams relentlessly in practice so that the game plan became second nature. And he meticulously scouted opponents, a skill that was evident in his practice before meeting Bird and Indiana State. He had Johnson practice with Michigan State's second team and told the first unit they should pretend that Johnson was Larry Bird. Johnson was instructed to do it all, pass, shoot, run, while Heathcote told the first unit to hound Magic-as-

Larry, double-team him, harass him, force him to give up the ball before he could make a play.

Heathcote was well aware that Bird could pick teams apart with his amazing passing skill. But, the best way for Bird to beat you was with his magnificent shooting. Heathcote wanted every shot Bird took to be a tough one. He wanted him to be pressured so quickly that every pass didn't lead to someone else's basket. Heathcote's strategy worked. Michigan State's defense wore down Bird and Indiana State, limiting him to 19 points (he was averaging 30) and only 2 assists. And with its defense keeping it close, Michigan State pulled away in the second half for a 75–64 victory and the NCAA title. Johnson meanwhile had 24 points, and he added 10 assists in a typically unselfish exhibition of leadership that won him the first round of what would be basketball's ultimate bout—Magic vs. Larry.

That first meeting did not result in memorable statistics for either Bird or Magic. But their first meeting alerted the nation to their skills. Those fans would follow them to the NBA, which at the time desperately needed new, attractive faces. The league had several teams that were losing money, and its national TV appeal was fading. The arrival of Magic and Larry changed all that. They brought to the NBA two of the most fascinating personalities and performers ever to play the game. These two players had already developed national followings who transferred their allegiance from college ball to professional basketball. Bird and Magic were huge attractions when they visited other NBA cities, as well as reenergizing their own teams, which just happened to be the league's most glamorous franchises, Los Angeles and Boston.

After that sophomore year in which he won the NCAA title, Magic decided he would make himself available to the pros. It had become evident that Los Angeles would use the first pick in the draft (acquired years previously as compensation for Gail Goodrich, who had left as a free agent to New Orleans) to select Johnson and team him with such established stars as Kareem Abdul-Jabbar, Norm Nixon, and Jamaal Wilkes. Johnson was only twenty, but he was obviously physically mature enough to play in the pros. And he did not want to risk injury by returning to Michigan State for another season. He would be able to go to one of basketball's glamour franchises for top dollar. He would be able to acquire a contract that would immediately ease his father's heavy workload and allow his mother to raise the rest of the family without financial worries.

So it was an easy decision for Magic when he announced six weeks after the NCAA title game that he would make himself available in the draft. Five days later, he was a member of the Lakers. And he would quickly show that he belonged in the NBA.

The NCAA title game created a national identity for Johnson and Bird. When Johnson's career is reviewed years from now, no one performance will likely be more revered than his first NBA championship at the end of his rookie season. He had already had a memorable first NBA year, starting on opening night. He was an irrepressible twenty-year-old, playing with men a dozen years older than he and bringing with him an enthusiasm and pure joy that were rare in the businesslike world of the pros. On opening night, Johnson made every highlight film on every sportscast in America when he leaped into the arms of a surprised Kareem Abdul-Jabbar after Jabbar's skyhook won the game that was Magic's nationally televised professional debut at the buzzer. Johnson would later become the first rookie in eleven years to start in an NBA All-Star game.

No one could resist Johnson's innocent charm, least of all his teammates, who responded to his unique abilities by sweeping into the NBA finals and a matchup with Julius Erving (the remarkable Dr. J) and the Philadelphia 76ers. Just a summer ago, Erving had offered Johnson, then a college freshman, some pointers. Johnson had played in a summer league tournament in Philadelphia, and Erving had taken Johnson under his wing. In particular, Dr. J. watched Johnson's rather unorthodox jump shot and suggested Johnson work on banking the ball off the glass. Magic took the advice, and during his rookie NBA season, his scoring repertoire largely consisted of bank shots, with his swooping lay-ups and jump hooks thrown in as well. Now Magic and the Doctor were meeting with a championship on the line.

The Lakers took a 3–2 lead in the series. But in the fifth game in Los Angeles, Jabbar sprained his ankle. He came back to play a great last quarter, holding off a late Sixers charge, which ended at the buzzer when Henry Bibby inadvertently stepped out of bounds trying a last-second three-point shot that could have tied the game. The series then returned to Philadelphia. Jabbar remained in Los Angeles because his ankle injury had badly stiffened, making it impossible for him to run. Often forgotten is the way Sixers coach Billy Cunningham had prepared his team as if Jabbar would play. Despite the Lakers' statements that Jabbar would be unavailable for Game 6 and wouldn't even fly to Philadelphia with his team, Cunningham believed that when game time arrived Jabbar would arrive. Cunningham was proved wrong when Jabbar remained in Los Angeles, where he waited and hoped he'd be ready for a Game 7, which seemed inevitable because of his absence.

Even the Lakers believed they would likely need to go to a seventh game, because without Jabbar their chances of beating the Sixers in Philadelphia were slim. However, one Laker believed otherwise—the twenty-year old rookie named Magic Johnson. He had first shown his teammates he was ready to pick up the slack for Jabbar when, on the Lakers' flight to Philadelphia, he had deliberately sat in the seat Jabbar usually took. Later, as the Lakers' bus was heading for the Philadelphia Spectrum, Johnson walked by Lakers coach Paul Westhead, winked, and said, "Don't worry about anything. I'll play center."

When the game began, fans at the Philadelphia Spectrum and those watching on television were shocked to see none other than Magic Johnson walking out to center court to jump center against Philadelphia's seven-foot Caldwell Jones. It was amazing enough throughout his rookie season to see Johnson rotate between point guard and power forward, a combination never before played by one man in the NBA. But now he was playing center, which was beyond belief. Johnson then proceeded to set the tone for one of basketball's most amazing evenings by getting the tap, receiving a return pass, and then swooping by Philadelphia's behemoth Darryl Dawkins for a swooping lay-up to open the game.

Magic played like a man possessed. No one could contain him, not Bobby Jones, who was considered the best defensive forward of his era, not Dr. J., not Maurice Cheeks, one of Johnson's toughest foes through the years, not Caldwell Jones, the 76ers' center, who actually guarded Johnson much of the time when he was filling the center spot.

Though that match is now remembered as the game he played center, Johnson actually played very little of the classic center position after the opening moments. He rarely went down low to post up a defender. Rather, with Caldwell Jones often guarding him, Johnson floated outside, where the Sixers seemed content to let him take jump shots. And Johnson repeatedly buried them, many times on the bank shot suggested by Dr. J. During the course of the amazing game, Magic eventually played every position on the floor—point guard, shooting guard, power forward, and small forward, as well as center. His personal numbers read like a box score from one of his Everett High School games—47 minutes, 42 points, 15 rebounds, 7 assists, 3 steals, 14 of 14 free throws, 14 of 23 field goals. But this wasn't Everett High School. This was for the National Basketball Association title, and it was a championship game performance that veteran NBA observers like Harvey Pollack, the longtime Philadelphia stats wizard, and reporters on the scene consider the greatest ever witnessed in such a big game. (Ironically, one that rivaled it was performed by Lakers general manager Jerry West. In a losing Game 7 effort in 1969, West scored 42 points along with 13 rebounds and 12 assists.)

Magic's personal scoring line was impressive enough. But what always made him special was the way he lifted his teammates to new levels of their own game, and so it was that remarkable day. Los Angeles forward Jamaal Wilkes scored 37 points while adding 10 rebounds. Guard Norm Nixon complemented Johnson in the backcourt. Michael Cooper came up with a big defensive effort against Erving. Reserve guard Brad Holland hit three big jump shots late in the game after the Sixers had come back from 12 points down to close to within a point. They had all hitched themselves to Johnson's Superman cape, and they went on a Magic-al ride that ended with a 123–107 Lakers victory, earning them their first title in eight years.

Johnson later told *Sports Illustrated* that one great memory indeed was Game 6 of the 1980 NBA finals against Philadelphia. "It was the most amazing game of my career," he said. "I've probably watched the tape of that game a thousand times. It's almost always in one or another of the VCRs in my house. Whenever I'm down, I watch that game."

In his innocence, Magic thought this was how it was supposed to be. You leave college after winning the NCAA title in your sophomore year, join the Lakers, and then win the NBA title in your rookie season. But only two other players had ever been part of NCAA champion teams and NBA champion teams in successive seasons—Bill Russell and Henry Bibby. And when you throw in Everett High's state championship, it meant that Johnson had been part of championship teams at three different levels in the space of four years. No player had ever achieved such a remarkable series of triumphs.

Johnson, of course, would finally taste reality in the coming years. He would suffer the first major injury of his career. He would suffer play-off humiliation. And he would have problems with a coach for the only time in his career, receiving rare criticism because of them.

Jack McKinney coached the Lakers to open the 1979–80 season. McKinney believed in an up-tempo game and allowed the Lakers to flow offensively, with Magic in control and free to pick and choose his offensive options. It was a philosophy made to order for Johnson's creative skills, as well as those of his Los Angeles teammates, who included great scoring weapons like Jabbar, Nixon, and Wilkes. McKinney's style would in fact be the system that would later become known as "Showtime," a philosophy that asked the Lakers to play fast-break court whenever given the chance and put the high-speed options in the hands of Magic Johnson.

However, twelve games into that rookie season, McKinney suffered a serious head injury in a bicycle accident and was replaced by Lakers assistant coach Paul Westhead. McKinney would never return to full-time coaching. It was a tragedy that Magic often lamented because he always felt grateful for the way McKinney had eased his transition from college to the pros at such a young age. Meanwhile, for the remainder of that season, Westhead maintained the system installed by McKinney, and it resulted in the Lakers' winning the world championship.

However, when training camp opened the next summer, Westhead informed the team that he was installing an all-new system. Whereas they were accustomed to a free-form style, Westhead demanded a rigid structure in which every time down the court was designed to run in a specific way. Those fast breaks that would be called Showtime were allowed, but if they didn't quickly result in a score, the Lakers were under orders to slow down and go back to Westhead's choreographed style. This rigid style quickly discouraged the Lakers. They were being forced to play completely out of character. Magic was the most affected. Asking him to walk up the ball in preset plays was like having Michael Jackson moonwalk to music by Lawrence Welk.

Although the Lakers still won most of their games because of their overwhelming talent, they became a joyless team. Shockingly, they were eliminated in the first round of playoffs by Houston and Moses Malone. Factors other than Westhead's coaching system contributed to the Lakers' demise that year. The team had problems dealing with being champions. Some veteran players felt they weren't large enough parts of the offense. For much of the year, it became a selfish team. Part of the reason might have been that Johnson was forced to miss forty games with a knee injury that required surgery. He wrote in *Magic's Touch* of his first major injury, "I was scared. I had some of the best doctors in the country and the only thing they could assure me was that they'd do everything possible to make my knee healthy again. But even after surgery and three months of strenuous rehabilitation, I still wondered if I would have the same knee, if I would be the same player. I didn't know if the knee would collapse again after a week, a month, a year or even ten years. It is not a good feeling for any young athlete to experience."

Johnson eventually returned in time for the Lakers' ill-fated stretch drive. But when they returned the next fall for what was Johnson's third season, Westhead installed the same system once again. A few weeks into the season, Johnson's frustrations finally spilled over in public. He declared he couldn't play in the current system and asked to be traded. The timing was unfortunate because before the season, Johnson had signed a much-publicized twenty-five-year, $25 million contract with the Lakers—at the time the most amazing deal ever made with an athlete. So it appeared to many that Johnson had made himself bigger than the team, an impression underscored soon after when Westhead was fired.

For the first and only time in his career, Johnson was perceived as a problem player, someone who resisted authority and had eventually gotten his coach fired. The characterization wounded Johnson, who had been brought up to respect authority and accept discipline and had blossomed under such strict coaches as George Fox and Jud Heathcote. Johnson would write in *Magic's Touch* that he would come to regret how he handled the Westhead situation. "I know now I should have kept my feelings to myself," he wrote. "I didn't mean for Westhead to be fired. I guess I was naive to think I would be traded before the coach was fired but at the time, I honestly was ready to play somewhere else."

Ironically Westhead went on to coach Loyola Marymount, where he installed the wildest run and gun offense in the history of college basketball. He later moved on to coach the Denver Nuggets and created a similar high-scoring, fastbreak offense. But the most significant offshoot of Westhead's firing was his replacement by Pat Riley, who had moved from the broadcast booth to be an assistant coach. As the Lakers' head man, with his expensive suits and slicked-back hair, he came to symbolize Showtime almost as much as one of Magic's forty-foot bounce passes.

Johnson's decision to speak out against Westhead ultimately helped create the Lakers' dynasty. At the time, he had appeared petulant and selfish. But much of his frustration stemmed from the Lakers not being allowed to play their best. To play their best required that he have the freedom to push the ball up the court and use his unparalleled creativity. All Magic ever wanted to do was have fun playing basketball and win. With Westhead's style the Lakers didn't have fun and they couldn't win. For twenty-two-year old Magic to recognize the problem and elect to speak out about it demonstrated that the boy was becoming a man of convictions.

4

Beating Boston

In recent years, it has seemed as if the irresistible allure of Magic Johnson vs. Larry Bird created what was the National Basketball Association's most glamorous rivalry—the Los Angeles Lakers vs. the Boston Celtics. There's no question that the rivalry between Johnson and Bird helped make Lakers-Celtics games the NBA's marquee attraction through the 1980s and into the early 1990s.

The truth is that Earvin Johnson and Larry Bird were infants when the rivalry between the Lakers and Celtics was born. The competition between the NBA titans rivaled the Red Sox vs.

the Yankees and the Dodgers vs. the Giants in baseball, the Bears vs. the Packers and the Cowboys vs. the Redskins in football. For nearly thirty years, Lakers-Celtics games have been the basketball version of Army-Navy.

When the teams met in the regular season, the games were special events. Even on those rare occasions when they'd meet in preseason exhibitions, there was a different feeling. Even now, a seasoned veteran like Bird openly looks forward to playing the Lakers. The matchups are always nationally televised, as was the Sunday afternoon in 1986 when the Lakers snapped the Celtics' forty-eight-game Boston Garden winning streak. As Johnson once said in an interview, "Whenever we play the Celtics, we could be in a playground and it would seem like we're playing in the last game to be played in basketball history. It didn't matter if we were playing in the Boston Garden with all those championship flags or at the Forum with all the limos and all the Hollywood stars."

The most memorable Lakers-Celtics duels always came in the NBA finals. What made this classic confrontation unique is that until Johnson came of age as a Los Angeles star, the bottom-line results were totally in Boston's favor. These duels involved some of basketball's most legendary players, like Bill Russell, Wilt Chamberlain, Bob Cousy, Elgin Baylor, Jerry West, John Havlicek, Sam Jones, and Gail Goodrich. But until Magic came along, Boston always broke the Lakers' hearts. From 1959 until 1984, there were twenty-five NBA finals. The Celtics and Lakers met an amazing eight of those times and, even more amazingly, Boston beat L.A. each and every time.

Along the way, the two teams would play some of the NBA's most epic games. There was the incredibly hard-fought 1962 championship series that went to a seventh game in Boston Garden. That game came down to the final seconds when, with the score tied, Lakers' guard Frank Selvy had a jump shot at the buzzer to win the game. It rimmed out and Russell leaped high to grab the rebound and then collapsed on the floor in complete exhaustion, sending the game into overtime. Russell was revived, and so were the Celtics—they went on to win by three points.

There was the playoff game a few years later in Boston when the incomparable Baylor scored 61 points while being guarded, as always, by Tom Sanders, considered one of the best defensive forwards ever. Unbelievably, the Celtics still won that game in which Baylor dominated. There was the night when the Celtics clinched another title as Cousy (whose magnificent ball-handling skills and passing wizardry were the ancestors of the skills Magic would bring to the NBA) dribbled out the last dozen seconds. Frustrated Lakers players were unable to catch the elusive Cousy in order to foul him and stop the clock. And as the final seconds ticked off, the Boston Garden crowd surged around the court, when the buzzer sounded engulfing Cousy in one of the wildest scenes in NBA history.

There was the clinching game in 1965 when Boston opened the fourth quarter by scoring 18 straight points en route to yet another championship. And then there was 1969, a season in which the aging Celtics finished fourth in their division and were given little chance of going anywhere in the playoffs. Somehow, they got to the Finals and a seventh game in Los Angeles. Lakers owner Jack Kent Cooke had hundreds of balloons suspended from the ceiling in anticipation of what seemed certain victory. But the Celtics hung close and the game turned in the final minutes on a Don Nelson shot that bounced three times on the rim before dropping straight through the basket to break the Lakers' hearts once again.

The rivalry, at least the one in the NBA finals, lapsed for fifteen years. But it was resumed with the arrival of Johnson in Los Angeles and Bird in Boston. They helped bring this duel into a new generation and lift it to new heights. They arrived together in the NBA for the 1979–80 season. For the entire decade thereafter, the NBA finals would always include at least one of the two teams. For many years, the battles were bitter and volatile. As Johnson once said, "For a long time, we thought the Celtics were cheapshot artists and we thought about nothing else but retaliation. It went on for years because we were both trying to establish ourselves as the best. If they took one of our guys out, then we had to do the same to one of theirs. It started getting very dangerous and it wasn't the way basketball should be played."

Eventually the Lakers and Celtics grew out of that behavior, but it took a while. It wasn't until the 1984 finals that Johnson and Bird had their first playoff collision. It resulted in one of the biggest disappointments of Johnson's playing life, which in turn would eventually write another chapter in the book of his courageous career.

The 1984 finals began with the first two games in Boston. The Lakers won the opener in the Garden, and they seemed to have Game 2 in hand as well. With seconds left, Los Angeles held a two-point lead. A victory would have meant they had swept the first two games in Boston and would have given them a stranglehold on the championship, with the finals heading back to Los Angeles. But it wasn't meant to be. Johnson failed under pressure as the game turned on one of his rare mistakes. James Worthy made an inbound pass which was intended for Magic, who could seal the game simply by receiving the ball. But Johnson did not come quickly to the ball, and the pass was stolen by Celtics guard Gerald Henderson, who then scored an easy lay-up to tie the game. With still time enough for a last shot, Johnson then took the inbound pass, but froze and did not advance the ball as time ran out, sending the game into overtime, where Boston would earn a 124–121 victory that tied the series.

Johnson would stand tall later, taking the blame for Henderson's interception. "I should have come to the ball but didn't," he said. "That was mostly my fault, not James's." Nevertheless, for one of the few times in his career, Johnson was criticized in the media for his play. Then, amazingly enough, a similar disaster unfolded two games later, in the fourth game.

Magic and Los Angeles came back to win the third game, with Johnson setting a NBA finals record by recording 21 assists. That was the same game in which Boston's Kevin McHale committed a vicious foul against the Lakers' Kurt Rambis, a physical play that came to represent the bitter history between the two teams. Emotions were high when in Game 4, the Lakers and Boston played another classic. With the score tied, Los Angeles had the ball with sixteen seconds left and called a time-out to set up what they hoped would be a game-winning play that would give them a 3–1 lead in the series. Center Kareem Abdul-Jabbar, who normally would have been the Lakers' first offensive option, had fouled out of the game. So the Lakers decided on a favorite two-man play in which Worthy would post up low and Johnson would be on the wing with the ball, having the option of passing into Worthy or making an offensive move for himself.

However, Johnson became uncharacteristically overcautious. Undecided about how to attack the Boston defense, he allowed too much time to go off the clock. Finally Johnson decided to pass into Worthy, but he lobbed the ball too softly. Celtics center Robert Parish knocked the soft pass away as time expired, sending the game into overtime. Magic's anguish became complete when, with the score tied and thirty-five seconds left in overtime, he missed two free throws. Bird then came down to score, the Lakers threw another pass away, and Boston had tied the series, 2–2. The Celtics eventually went on to win the series in seven games.

Johnson thus had a direct hand in the two crucial losses of the series. He wrote in *Magic's Touch* that the summer after that playoff defeat was the "worst of my life. It was the lowest point of my career." He took direct responsibility for losing another championship to the hated Celtics, and some Lakers thought his career would be permanently scarred by the disappointment. Lakers general manager Jerry West went so far as to say that he feared Johnson would never recover from the criticism he received after the 1984 failure.

But instead of scarring Johnson, the experience made him an even better player and better man. Johnson accepted his failure and vowed not to let it repeat itself. Years later, in his battle with the HIV virus, Johnson again would use adversity to become a stronger person. Instead of avoiding responsibility in the years after the 1984 playoff defeat to Boston, Johnson went out of his way to shoulder more of the load and take even more pressure upon himself. In the process, he again lifted his entire team to new heights.

The bitter 1984 defeat was fresh on the Lakers' minds when they began the next season. Some Lakers still shook with the memory of the wild scene in Boston at the end of the 1984 series. During Games 1 and 2 of the series, the Lakers had been forced to switch Boston hotels when fire alarms constantly woke them up. On the day of the seventh game, the Lakers needed a police escort to escape their hotel and board their bus for their pregame workout. On the morning of the seventh game, Boston fans had blocked the hotel entrance, and Boston police needed attack dogs and motorcycle escorts to ensure the Lakers' safety. Later that night, after the Boston victory, the Garden turned ugly, with fans hurling trash at Lakers players and then attacking them in the postgame melee. Other fans threw rocks at the Lakers' bus as it finally escaped the Garden after the seventh-game defeat.

The Garden itself had become like a haunted house for the Lakers. The ancient building is professional basketball's most hallowed shrine, with the Celtics' championship banners covering the grimy ceiling along with the retired numbers of former greats. The Garden looks a lot better on television than it does in person.

Numerous dead spots dot the famous parquet floor, resulting in mis-bounces of the ball that often cause seasoned players to lose their dribbles. The visitors' locker room is roughly the size of a large closet, and the Celtics have been suspected of turning the heat up to sauna levels or, in the winter, making it feel like a refrigerator. The arena has no air conditioning, and the Lakers still remembered the night during one playoff series when unseasonable weather caused temperatures to reach nearly 100 degrees on the court. There are dozens of opposing players, not to mention average fans, who will swear to spotting rats the size of small dogs inhabiting the dark, ancient corridors.

The Garden factor was part of the Celtics' mystique, especially in the wake of the violent end to the 1984 series. The Lakers approached the 1985 season as if on a mission. That was especially true for Johnson, who knew full well that his failures in Games 2 and 4 largely cost Los Angeles a chance to beat Boston in the playoffs for the first time. He wanted nothing more than to bring the Lakers back to the finals against Boston. And inevitably, the 1985 NBA season eventually came down to the end the world demanded and Magic had dreamed of. For the ninth time, the Celtics and Lakers played off for the championship.

The opener was ominous for Los Angeles. With heightened security making the Boston Garden less like the war zone of a year ago, the Celtics inflicted an epic Game 1 loss on the Lakers. Boston set a record for points in a championship game, pounding Los Angeles by the incredible score of 148–114. Fortunately for the Lakers, they had three days between games to recuperate from the rout. Johnson and his teammates finally took a stand against Boston. They won Game 2 in the Garden and went on to win the championship, clinching it with a sixth-game victory made doubly sweet by winning in Boston. Kareem Abdul-Jabbar was the Series Most Valuable Player, but it was Johnson who held the Lakers together after the awful first game, playing error-free throughout the series and running the show as only he could.

Finally, the Lakers had shed the awful Celtics burden. For the first time, they had beaten Boston in the NBA finals, and they had done it in the hostile confines of Boston Garden. As Johnson said later, "The sweetest sound I ever heard was the quiet in the Garden when we took over the sixth game of the 1985 Finals. Sometimes, it would be so loud in there that we couldn't hear Pat Riley's voice in our huddle. But in the last minutes, it went from thousands of people yelling for us to lose to just quiet."

The 1985 Series, while finally ending Boston's longstanding dominance, also changed the way in which the two teams viewed each other. They seemed to have played above the violence and cheap shots and achieved a mutual respect that was unprecedented in professional sports. Much of that change in feeling stemmed from the growing personal closeness between Magic and Larry, a unique friendship. The team and the players still tried their best to beat each other. The competition was as fierce as any in professional sports. But each team had learned to respect howthe other played. They grew to have pride in themselves and in their rivalry, and that pride seemed to make them want to play the game minus the bitterness and cheap shots.

Sadly for the NBA, the Celtics and Lakers would meet only once more in the Magic-Larry era. That came in the 1987 finals when Magic turned around the series in Los Angeles's favor. He did it with what he has called the most memorable shot of his career. Again the scene was Boston Garden, and again Magic demonstrated his willingness to shoulder the load for his team. It was Game 4 with the Lakers holding a 2–1 lead but trailing the Celtics by a point with eight seconds left. Johnson got the ball outside. His first thought was dumping the ball inside to Jabbar, who was guarded by Parrish. However, Boston forward Kevin McHale came outside to guard Johnson, and Magic knew he had the quickness to get around McHale.

Then, as Johnson began wheeling around McHale, Parrish took a step out to try and block the path. Magic pirouetted and flipped up a hook shot, reminiscent on a smaller scale of Jabbar's patented skyhook. The shot arced over the hands of both Parrish and McHale and swished through the net. The roar of the Boston Garden crowd fell into a tomb-like silence, punctuated only by the screams of the fifteen Lakers celebrating Johnson's amazing clutch play and the victory that would eventually lead to Los Angeles's winning the title in six games. It also culminated what might have been Magic's best season, a year in which he was named both playoff MVP and NBA Most Valuable Player for the regular season.

The Lakers would follow up that 1987 title with another in 1988 for the first back-to-back NBA title in nineteen years since the Celtics had won consecutive titles. Los Angeles' 1988 title came against Detroit, however, and during their celebration, some Lakers would say that winning a title without having to beat Boston almost seemed a little empty. There's likely no better indication of what this wonderful Celtics-Lakers rivalry meant to both teams. Indeed, in the weeks preceding Magic's retirement, both Johnson and Bird told reporters that with their careers winding down, they'd love nothing more than to have the Celtics and Lakers meet one more time with an NBA title on the line.

It is no mere coincidence that the Lakers finally ended their long, grim jinx against the Celtics with Magic leading the way. He was able to do what West and Baylor and Chamberlain and all the others couldn't do, namely carry the Lakers to victory past Boston. Magic did it after coming back from the 1984 mistakes that had been the lowest point of his career. He had shown the courage to turn around that adversity and eventually overcome it by leading the Lakers to two titles over the hated Celtics.

5

Winning Time

No team was ever more dominant in its sport than the Boston Celtics of the late 1950s and 1960s. Led by the incomparable Bill Russell, the Celtics won eleven NBA titles in an amazing thirteen-year period. In the two years when they didn't win the championship, Russell had been injured in the playoffs.

Given how modern teams rarely stay on top for such a length of time, it seems hard to imagine another individual or team approaching such a long reign of excellence. The exception in recent years has been Magic Johnson. In his twelve-year career with the Los Angeles Lakers, Johnson came close to matching Russell's amazing winning tradition. There is reason to believe that Johnson's record of five titles and nine appearances in the finals over those dozen seasons is as impressive as Russell's record, given the difference in eras.

Certainly Russell's achievement or the caliber of player during his time cannot be diminished. The great players of Russell's era—Russell himself, Wilt Chamberlain, Bob Cousy, Elgin Baylor, Oscar Robertson, Bob Pettit, Jerry West, Nate Thurmond, and all the others—would have been greats no matter when they played. Certainly no matter what the level of competition, any team which won as regularly as the Boston teams is remarkable and a tribute to Russell's and the Celtics' incredible competitive fury.

A strong case, however, can be made that the level of play every night in today's NBA has never been tougher. The size and athleticism of the players, the depth of talent, and the players' conditioning are far beyond what they were twenty-five years ago. The cross-country travel takes a brutal toll on modern players.

Even the lowliest NBA teams have three or four great scorers. The defense in every game is stronger than it's ever been. While sports like baseball worry about losing talented athletes, basketball is overflowing with them. It is the one sport that has been turning in more highly skilled players every year, with no end in sight. Whether it is the complacency of today's millionaire athletes or simply the depth of overall talent, rare indeed are professional champions who enjoy extended stays at the top. All of which makes Magic's nine finals in twelve seasons with the Lakers one of the most remarkable achievements of this generation.

That still doesn't make Magic's Lakers career the equal of Russell's. But Magic Johnson is one of the few players who deserves the honor of being mentioned in the same sentence with Russell as one of professional basketball's biggest winners.

One reason Magic has been able to remain on top was that he always refused to allow disappointments to linger. Whenever he experienced a defeat or injury, he came back better than before. He has the uncanny ability not only to make others play better, but also to raise his game to whatever level is needed to win. A trip year by year through Magic's career reveals a series of high points and very few lows. Even those occasional low points inspired Johnson and his Lakers to new triumphs. As Magic said in his book *Magic's Touch*, "When I'm playing basketball, I'm playing to win, nothing else. Not to score, to rebound or to excel in one particular area of the game but to win."

For example, after he had knee surgery early in the 1980–81 season, he returned 45 games later to average nearly 23 points a game down the stretch. Then came the Lakers' quick exit from the playoffs, followed by the controversial beginning of the 1981–82 season, when Lakers coach Paul Westhead was fired in a move that seemed largely to have been instigated by Johnson's resistance to Westhead's coaching style. For one of the few times in Johnson's career, he was viewed as the bad guy. How did he respond? With new coach Pat Riley reinstalling the Lakers' running attack and making Johnson again the floor leader, the Lakers proceeded to roll into the NBA finals by becoming the first NBA team ever to sweep consecutive series without a loss. They capped their playoff run by defeating Philadelphia for the NBA title, with Magic winning his second playoff MVP award. By then, those Lakers fans who might have felt Johnson had overstepped his position by influencing the firing of Westhead had long forgotten the details surrounding the coaching change.

After the 1982 title, the Lakers went to the finals in each of the next two seasons, losing both times. One defeat came at the hands of the Philadelphia 76ers, who were led by center Moses Malone and forward Julius Erving, whom Johnson looked up to as his hero. The next year Los Angeles lost to Boston in the crushing 1984 series, when Johnson's mistakes in Games 2 and 4 were the turning points. However, despite those disappointments in the NBA finals, Johnson had become unquestionably the NBA's biggest star. In 1983, he was voted for the first time to the All-NBA first team. It would be the first of nine straight honors. In 1985, he received 957,000 votes in the All-Star balloting by fans, a league record and an indication of the affection fans had for him, not only in Los Angeles but all over the country. Magic then rewarded his fans that year with a 21-point, 15-assist All-Star game masterpiece.

In 1985 came the sweetest NBA title for Johnson and the Lakers as they finally ended Boston's long playoff domination by beating the Celtics in the NBA finals. However, the next year proved to be one of those rare disappointments. The Lakers were eliminated early in the NBA playoffs by Houston, ending a season that Johnson later said was a year when the Lakers' egos wouldn't let them repeat as champions, a season that ended in some controversy because of the clubhouse discontent. Subsequently, Coach Riley challenged Johnson to come back the next season and not only play the floor general, but also add to his scoring. As always, Johnson responded to the challenge by coming back in 1986–87 with what might have been his greatest season. Along the way, he helped the Lakers break Boston's 48-game home winning streak, achieved his career scoring high with a 46-point performance against Sacramento, scored his 10,000th career point, achieved a career-high 23.9 scoring average for the season, had one incredible and unprecedented streak of four consecutive triple-doubles (games in which he had double figures in points, rebounds, and assists), and finally beat Boston for another NBA title while winning MVP awards for both the regular season and the play-offs.

For an encore, Johnson and the Lakers came back to win it all in 1988. They thus became the first team to repeat as champions since the Celtics in 1969. However, by now the physical strain of playing nearly 40 minutes a game for more than 100 games a year was beginning to show. Johnson had for years been bothered by tendinitis in his knees, and they often ached. He grew much more attentive to off-season conditioning, adding running and cycling and weight work while also adopting many of the stretching exercises that helped teammate Kareem Abdul-Jabbar play in the NBA longer than any man in history. Still, Johnson had one of his toughest injury years ever in 1989. A pulled hamstring forced him to sit out in the 1989 All-Star game. Another hamstring injury in Game 2 of the 1989 finals sidelined him the rest of the way as Detroit swept the Lakers to prevent Los Angeles from achieving a three-peat—three straight titles.

Then the Lakers failed to reach the finals in 1990, though Magic would win another MVP award, his third in four years. Many NBA observers believed the Lakers might be a club on the decline. Jabbar had retired after the 1989 season, and some thought it was more than a coincidence that the Lakers failed to get to the finals in their first season without him. Johnson was now over thirty, with an increasingly aching body that was showing the wear and tear of averaging thirty-seven minutes per game for his entire career, plus long playoff series that in effect had added more than two full NBA seasons to his career.

But 1990–91 would be very special for Johnson. Late in the season, with his father in attendance, he broke Oscar Robertson's record for career assists. "It was a record I cherished very much because it was such a great honor," said Johnson. "And it is something that pays tribute to all the great passers who came before me."

The assist record stands beside Magic's string of appearances in NBA finals as the numbers that define him as a player. "Magic Johnson and Bob Cousy were the two greatest passers ever to play this game," said Red Auerbach, the legendary boss of the Boston Celtics. "There's never been anybody who ran the fastbreak like they did. They would always hit the right man at the right time. They would play the game the right way. They rewarded the guys who worked hard to get the rebound by getting the ball in position to score. Both of them could score themselves but both Magic and Cousy thought pass first.

"Cousy had the assist record for a time and then it was broken by Oscar [Robertson]. But it's justice that if Cousy can't have it, then Magic should be the one who does."

Indeed, passing always had been the one constant with Johnson. Throughout his career, he used whatever parts of his game were needed in a particular game or season. For example, in his early years with the Lakers, they didn't need his scoring because they had Jabbar in his prime and Jamaal Wilkes and Norm Nixon and other excellent scorers. What the Lakers needed were Johnson's on-court direction, his leadership, and his enthusiasm. Later, Riley told Johnson that the Lakers needed more scoring, and Johnson responded by becoming more of a scorer, adding the three-point shot to his repertoire. When Jabbar retired, Johnson would often take up some of the slack inside by posting up his man and using his excellent hook and close-to-the-basket moves in leading the Lakers to the finals without Kareem in both 1989 and 1991.

Through it all, the constant was Magic sharing the ball with his teammates and making them better players. No matter what else he was called upon to do, his unselfishness and leadership were the backbone of the Lakers and of the way Johnson played. Johnson appeared to have years left in his career. His contract ran through the 1993–94 season, and he had hinted he wouldn't mind playing beyond that if his knees held up and he still felt the same enthusiasm for the game. As well, he seemed rejuvenated by having taken the Lakers to another NBA final in 1991, even though they were swept by Michael Jordan and the Chicago Bulls. It appeared that Magic had several productive seasons left.

Before his sudden retirement due to the HIV virus shattered the Lakers just three games into the 1991–92 NBA season, Johnson had high hopes for the Lakers. Days before the season was scheduled to begin and before he had learned the awful news, he talked to Lakers general manager Jerry West and was brimming with confidence. "He told me that he had been reading all the predictions about the Lakers being the third-best team in the West behind Portland and San Antonio, and Magic was laughing," said West. "He told me this was going to be one of the best teams we ever had. He couldn't wait for the season to begin."

Los Angeles had never replaced Jabbar with a true dominant center. However, the team had a blend of big, mobile people. James Worthy remained one of the league's best offensive players, as did guard Byron Scott. Sam Perkins had fit right in and was blossoming as a major scorer. Center Vlade Divac continued to improve. The Laker bench looked much stronger with emerging young players Tony Smith and Elden Campbell. There was the addition of guard Sedale Threatt, who with Smith would be able to give the thirty-two-year-old Johnson a little rest. He could no longer average those thirty-seven minutes a game and be expected to lead a running team. Los Angeles had, in fact, by necessity run much less in 1991 because Magic simply couldn't keep up the pace. They wanted to return to Showtime, and their improved depth seemed to indicate it could be done. The Lakers felt a title was certainly possible for 1992. They had reached the NBA finals the year before and to a

Magic in 1978 as a freshman at Michigan State shows the thrilling form that would make him world-famous.
(Copyright © by AP/Wide World Photos)

Michigan State coach Jud Heathcote was a major influence in Magic's life. He taught him the importance of discipline on and off the court.
(Copyright © by AP/Wide World Photos)

►

Larry Bird gives Magic a hand during their famous meeting in the 1979 NCAA title game. They would go on to become fierce rivals and best friends.
(Copyright © by AP/Wide World Photos)

Magic during his sophomore year at Michigan State. He would lead the Spartans to the NCAA title.
(Copyright © by AP/Wide World Photos)

Johnson swoops down the lane before dishing off to Jabbar for one of Magic's all-time record 9,921 career assists. (Copyright © by AP/Wide World Photos)

◄

In his rookie season, Magic (right) and Kareem Abdul-Jabbar (left) harass Philadephia's Caldwell Jones (center) during the 1980 NBA finals. Later in the same series, Johnson would score 42 points in the championship game to lead the Lakers to the NBA title. (Copyright © by AP/Wide World Photos)

Even Magic made a mistake once in a while. Here he loses control of the ball while driving against Portland in 1990, when Portland would eliminate the Lakers from the NBA playoffs. (Copyright © by AP/Wide World Photos)

◄

It's "Showtime" as Magic makes one of the amazing no-look passes for which he was so famous. (Copyright © by AP/Wide World Photos)

Johnson proudly holds one of the three NBA Most Valuable Player Awards he won in his career. (Copyright © by AP/Wide World Photos)

►

Sitting this one out. Actually, this is a youthful Magic in a wheelchair basketball game held for charity. Johnson raises millions every year for worthy causes. (Copyright © by AP/Wide World Photos)

Ouch! Magic grimaces with pain after a collision under the basket. He had his share of injuries but still played over 1,000 NBA games. (Copyright © by AP/Wide World Photos)

Johnson shows a youngster how it's done at a clinic in Spain. Magic has far-flung commercial and business interests that have amassed a personal fortune of over fifty million dollars. (Copyright © by AP/Wide World Photos)

◄
Celebrating an NBA title with Lakers owner Dr. Jerry Buss. Johnson dreams of someday buying the Lakers.
(Copyright © by AP/Wide World Photos)

Larry Bird (center) tries to keep his composure in the Boston Garden during a moment of silent support for Johnson the night after he announced his retirement. (Copyright © by AP/Wide World Photos)

Magic talks with Arsenio Hall in his first appearance after announcing he had been infected with the HIV virus. (Copyright © by AP/Wide World Photos)

◄
Johnson poses in Paris, France, where he played last fall in what would be his last competition before learning he had been infected with the HIV virus. (Copyright © by AP/Wide World Photos)

Magic and Michael Jordan pose with their U.S. Olympic team jerseys. Johnson still hopes he can play in the Olympics despite his illness. (Copyright © by AP/Wide World Photos)

Michael Jordan, one of Johnson's best friends, was grim after learning that Magic had the HIV virus. (Copyright © by AP/Wide World Photos)

Led by A. C. Green, Johnson's Lakers teammates, along with members of the Phoenix Suns, offer prayers for Magic. The Lakers are struggling for some way to replace their leader. (Copyright © by AP/Wide World Photos)

Magic Johnson faces his biggest challenge with the same warmth and grace with which he's conducted himself throughout his outstanding career. (Copyright © by AP/Wide World Photos)

man, they felt they were better entering the 1991–92 season.

But then Johnson was lost as a player. The pain won't leave the Lakers for a long time. If ever a player in any sport was irreplaceable, it was Magic. On the court, no one could duplicate his blend of passing, scoring, size, and court sense. Beyond the loss of Magic's physical gifts, there was the loss of his leadership. There was no question in the Lakers' locker room who ran the show. This was Magic's team, pure and simple. And it had been for a dozen years.

"We have to go out there and do a job, but it's not going to be fun for a long while," said Scott. "You see guys in the finals in tears of agony after losing, but I've never been through anything like this. Part of me is gone. I look around on the court, over to where he's supposed to be, and then I think, 'wait, he's not here.' It's hard to find a way to stay with it."

Jabbar had written in his book *Kareem* about what it was like in 1989 when the Lakers had to play the last two games of the final series against Detroit without Johnson. "It's as if you had a great sports car and a great driver and all of a sudden you had to look to a guy that's been driving a bus to drive the car. It's pretty tough."

The harsh realities are that the Lakers went from being one of the league's best three or four teams with Johnson to a middle-of-the-road team without him. They went from being a team that might have won sixty games and been a serious contender for the NBA title to a forty- or forty-five-win team that dropped to that middle class of decent teams that are only long shots to go all the way. With the retirement of Johnson, the Lakers suddenly were transformed. Instead of being one of professional sport's glamour teams and a hot ticket everywhere they played, they had become one of the dozen or so pretty good NBA teams. When Magic retired, the Lakers not only lost their leader, they also lost their show-biz glitter, and that will be felt in Los Angeles and all over the NBA. As San Antonio forward Terry Cummings said, "The Lakers will never be the same team and the NBA will never be the same league."

The proud Lakers franchise tried to press on, but its executives realized that they had suffered a wound for which there was no remedy. "This is a terrible, terrible blow to our team from a playing standpoint," said general manager Jerry West. "You almost feel hopeless. We lost a great player, but the other things you can't replace are the ability to lead, the courage, the charisma. I think that somewhere out there, there's a young little kid who will be as great as Magic Johnson. But he won't be as great a leader."

Indeed, no one could calculate what Johnson meant to the Lakers. Said Perkins, "Magic was eighty-five percent of our team." A few years ago, Riley weighed what the Lakers would be like without Magic. At the time, he was discussing the impending retirement of Jabbar. Riley said that while it would be difficult to replace Jabbar, the team would have to change direction and it was something that was possible. Just then Magic walked by and someone asked Riley, "What about when Magic retires?" Riley stared at Johnson as he began taking some practice shots, and the Lakers coach replied, "When Magic retires, it's time for all of us to go home."

But the Lakers can't go home. They have to fight through their grief and try to compete in the tough world of the NBA. West mulled ways to improve the club in the wake of Johnson's retirement. In the days immediately after Johnson's departure, Threatt was thrust into a starting role at a point guard position he had rarely played before. However, no one on earth could replace Magic. "How do you make up for the loss of a great, great player any time, much less something that happens quickly like this?" said West. "It can't be done."

A large part of Magic's legend revolves around his rookie season, when he stepped in for injured Kareem Abdul-Jabbar in the sixth game of the 1980 NBA finals, played center and scored 42 points to lead the Lakers to an amazing championship victory. The story goes that flying from Los Angeles to Philadelphia for that game, Magic brazenly sat in Jabbar's seat on the Lakers' team plane, as if to reassure his teammates that he would take care of everything.

On the Lakers' flight home from Phoenix after their first game following Magic's retirement, his seat remained empty. It's likely that it will never be filled.

6

Larry, Michael Isiah, and Friends

When Magic Johnson announced his retirement from the Los Angeles Lakers after learning he had tested HIV positive, he left the door open for a return to playing basketball by fulfilling his ambition to play on the 1992 U.S. Olympic team. The one championship in his sport that Magic had never won was an Olympic gold medal.

Johnson still dreams of playing in the Olympics for more than a chance to win the medal. It has more to do with the prospect of playing on the same team with the other greats of his time, most of whom he has come to form close relationships with that are unique in professional sports. As Johnson told *Sports Illustrated,* "If I'm healthy, I might very well be on the floor for the opening tap in Barcelona. I agreed to play in the Olympics because I wanted to be there for my country, something I'd never been able to do before. I wanted to play on the same team as Michael and Larry, something that would give me the kind of high that . . . man! I get goose bumps just thinking about what it would be like to be on the floor with those guys."

Few stars of any sport have had as special a relationship with their bitterest on-court rivals. That closeness to rivals is part of Magic's basketball legacy that will last forever. Before his dramatic press conference to announce his retirement, Johnson first made phone calls to five close friends. One was his former Lakers coach, Pat Riley, now the coach of the New York Knicks, and another was to a Los Angeles buddy, Arsenio Hall, the popular actor and talk-show host. Those calls were easy to explain. But what was remarkable were the names of the other three individuals who received phone calls that torturous afternoon. The recipients were the stars of the last three teams Magic faced in the NBA finals—Boston's Larry Bird, Detroit's Isiah Thomas, and Chicago's Michael Jordan.

Such friendship with opponents is virtually unheard of in sports. Modern professional athletes are by nature self-centered, to the point where nowadays they rarely form close friendships even with teammates. To reach the top of this most competitive of professions, you must be completely absorbed in your own performance. You must spend countless hours working to improve your shooting or lifting weights to increase your strength or running mile after lonely mile to develop your endurance. The top athletes are usually viewed as being special early in life. From their teenage days, they are often coddled. They don't have to worry about buying sneakers; they're given to them. Chores are done for them, doors are opened for them. They are celebrities in their own local worlds, and if they make it to the pros, they become celebrities everywhere. That insulated existence inevitably fosters an egotism that makes it difficult to share the spotlight or praise another player or even be friendly with someone at the same plateau for fear of lessening the attention to oneself.

Beyond that, many of today's athletes have little sense of their sport's history or their place in the game's big picture. They are largely concerned with the moment, with how the team plays in the next game or how much money will be made in the next contract. They rarely have an appreciation of the truth that the best players are really only caretakers for sports that have been played for a century, that the sport has become a huge part of millions of people's lives, and that the sport will live long after today's superstars have retired.

Magic has always been different. On the one hand, he has always been the ultimate team player. Michigan State was Magic's team. And the Lakers were Magic's team. Their every move seemed to be orchestrated by Magic. The ball was always his to distribute where he felt best or shoot himself if necessary. No one had a more unquenchable thirst for winning. He would elbow his friend Isiah Thomas to the floor in pursuit of a loose ball or wrestle with Larry Bird for rebounding position or hound Michael Jordan all the way up the court with a big hand in his back.

Off the court, Johnson created an atmosphere around the Lakers that was unlike the atmosphere surrounding most other teams. He was the team leader, and because he treated everyone else with the same friendship, the Lakers never had cliques. They were unusually close off the court. As Johnson always said about his teammates, "We don't all have to be best friends with each other but when the game starts, everybody wearing a Lakers uniform is my brother."

However, by the midpoint in his career, Magic seemed to begin transcending merely being part of one team. Instead, he seemed to have become NBA basketball, an ambassador for the league and the game. He seemed to embody the Way the Game Should Be Played. Jordan and others could perform more amazing athletic feats. Other players were better than Magic in individual facets of the game, like rebounding or shooting. But Magic's way was the best way to play. He seemed to become a caretaker for the sport, not only to make his teammates better but to leave the game better than it was before he arrived.

He did it in so many ways. He made sure that the efforts of workmen like former Lakers forward Kurt Rambis were appreciated, that their effort to do the dirty work of rebounding and being physical under the boards was always noted. He made passing the ball something youngsters wanted to emulate; he made unselfish play the trendy way to play the game. Magic also reached out for friendship with the game's other contemporary greats, as if they all belonged to the most exclusive of fraternities, to which the basketball gods had entrusted their game for safekeeping.

No two people could be more different than Magic Johnson and Larry Bird. Magic grew up as a city kid in a black urban neighborhood where he learned his basketball on playgrounds. Larry grew up in French Lick, Indiana, a small-town boy who shot baskets near a field. Magic is Mr. Personality, always wearing a show-biz smile, as comfortable making the Hollywood scene as playing his brand of flashy ball. Larry is not a public personality; he plays the game with amazing subtlety and feels out of place in glitzy atmospheres. Magic has always been a Laker and Larry has always been a Celtic. One might think that they wouldn't give each other the time of day.

Early in his career, Bird lost patience with the media's constant comparisons between himself and Johnson. Bird and Johnson had been linked in the public's mind ever since their epic meeting in the 1979 NCAA final. Bird seemed unwilling to appreciate their place in the game's history. He was consumed with his own game. However, during the later years of their careers, the two formed a bond that rivals the link between the closest of boyhood friends or teammates. Bird spent two days in seclusion after Johnson called him with the news of his infection with the HIV virus.

"It doesn't seem fair, it doesn't seem right," said Bird. "If I had an idol, it would be Magic. He played the game the way I want to play it. He's been an enemy and a friend, a competitor."

Bird in recent years never hid his admiration for Johnson. Even when most fans and players considered Michael Jordan the game's premier player, Bird would always make Magic his first choice. "I've never seen a player as good as him," said Bird. "And there'll probably be nobody down the road as good as him. Other guys might come along who can score and rebound. But there'll never be anybody who can control the game like he does."

Both Johnson and Bird always hoped they'd meet one more time in the finals. As Bird told *Sports Illustrated* before the news of Johnson's retirement, "It's amazing when you think back to the years it was always us and them in the Finals. We kind of took it for granted. I don't think it's that way anymore. I think we appreciate what we had. The Finals is what we're working for. It would be a big accomplishment for us, no matter who we got in against. But it'd be sort of nice to get to play the Lakers again. That'd be fun, me and Magic again."

In the same *Sports Illustrated* story, it was related that the magazine was working on a story about the NBA stars who would be playing for the U.S. Olympic team. Magic would not agree to pose for the cover photo unless Bird was included. Johnson was informed that Bird at the time had no interest in playing in the Olympics. But Johnson insisted on making several phone calls to make sure that Bird would not be offended if Magic and not Bird appeared in the photo. Bird, in his unassuming way, didn't care. He has since changed his mind and will be part of the Olympics. But the incident underscores the two players' unique respect for each other.

Johnson always called his duel with the Bird "the best rivalry in sports." Magic yearned for one more playoff meeting with Bird. "It would be what everyone would want to see, one more time for old time's sake," Johnson would say. When Bird was out much of two seasons, first with heel injuries and then with back problems, Johnson felt the loss. "I would get up every morning for years and the first thing I'd look for in the paper was to see what Larry did the night before," said Johnson. "When he was out, I missed that, I missed following how he was doing."

Johnson felt his relationship with his old rival

Bird was more special than any other he developed. But he had other close friendships with some of the game's biggest stars and his biggest rivals. One was with Detroit's Isiah Thomas, with whom he dueled in the 1988 and 1989 NBA finals. The two didn't have the longstanding competitive bond which tied Magic with Bird. Thomas and Johnson never played against each other until they were in the NBA. But the two grew up in similar inner-city situations, and as Johnson put it in his book *Magic's Touch*, "the more we talked, the more we realized how much alike we were, how many secrets we shared." The pair are such close friends that when Thomas's Detroit Pistons visit Los Angeles, Thomas stays at Johnson's house. However, the two also agreed that would not be a good idea when the Pistons and Lakers met in the 1988 finals. It was in the first game of that series that the two met at midcourt before the game-opening jump ball and kissed each other on the check in a gesture Johnson called "a salute to our friendship and our respect for the game." Much was made of the unique moment, but no one questioned either player's intensity. Early in that first game, for example, Johnson elbowed Thomas to the floor as the Pistons guard tried to drive toward the basket.

Johnson developed similar closeness with rivals like Jordan, who decided to play in the Olympics only after Johnson urged him to. Magic wanted the team to comprise the best and brightest of America's basketball. He wanted a chance to play with the best, and that meant the team had to include Jordan. Indeed, when Johnson called Jordan with the news about the HIV virus, Jordan tried to lighten the moment by saying, "I guess you've gone and messed up the Olympic thing."

Philadelphia's Charles Barkley is another friend of Johnson's, who announced he would change his number from 34 to Magic's 32 as a tribute. Such mutual admiration is rare in any profession, much less athletics. It is a spirit that in a large measure was created by Magic.

This mutual respect among opponents has helped the NBA's brightening public image. The NBA is the one league that seems to be populated by players who appreciate the game they play. There appears to be a closeness among players that is missing from other sports. That closeness was underscored in the days after Johnson's retirement, when players from every team expressed shock and sadness at the news. It seemed inevitable that the NBA players would join together and make a major financial and educational effort in connection with the AIDS virus. Some of the reaction was likely due to the players' own fears about the HIV virus in the wake of Johnson's revelation. But there was also a genuine respect for Magic as a person and for his contributions to the game.

There is little doubt that Magic Johnson's legacy to basketball will live as long as the game is played.

For one thing, he forever changed the role of big men. No one else his size ever was able to do the things on a basketball court Magic did. Until Magic arrived, six-foot, nine-inch players were centers or forwards. Magic was the same height as Bill Russell, who many believe is the greatest center who ever lived. Players that big didn't handle the ball, didn't flip no-look passes while dribbling on the fast break, didn't orchestrate entire offenses and direct traffic. Players that big rebounded and scored from inside. There had been tall guards before, players like six-foot, seven-inch George Gervin, but they were scorers, not point guards like Magic.

Magic made it acceptable for big players to develop all their skills, not just inside scoring and rebounding. "His greatest contribution is that he freed up the mind of every big man," said George Raveling, the University of Southern California coach. "Big men were always discouraged from handling the ball or improving their ball handling skills. Magic demonstrated that they could handle the ball.

"And he revolutionized the game. He made a significant change in the mental approach of the game. He made other superstars better. Whoever he played with, he made them better."

Johnson's arrival on the scene signaled the emergence onto the court of bigger, more versatile and athletic players. Big men, players like

Clyde Drexler, Dominique Wilkins, Sean Elliott, Willie Anderson, and rookie Billy Owens, are doing things unheard of for players their size fifteen years ago. Johnson also signaled a trend toward having larger, more mobile players being able to shift between different positions. Indeed, upon Jabbar's retirement the Lakers were moving toward such a club. They had Johnson, as well as players like six-foot, nine-inch James Worthy, six-foot, nine-inch A. C. Green, six-foot, eight-inch Sam Perkins, six-foot, ten-inch Vlade Divac, six-foot, five-inch Byran Scott, and six-foot, six-inch Terry Teagle, all of whom were mobile enough and able to handle the ball well enough to interchange between guard, forward, and in most cases center.

However, Johnson's contribution to basketball isn't just his size. He became the first point guard to dominate the game. He made it cool to pass the ball, not just shoot it. Thousands of kids all over the world worked on no-look passes and forty-foot bounce passes instead of dunks or jump shots. He made unselfish play the way to play the game, a legacy that coaches everywhere embraced. As Julius Erving once said, "Magic is the only player ever who could take only three shots and still dominate a game."

Coach Pat Riley also pointed to Johnson's fundamentally sound style of play. Riley always called Johnson either Earvin or Buck and always thought that the "Magic" nickname in a way gave the wrong impression. "He was never as fancy as people thought," Riley said. "He has instead always been a fundamentally sound player who never did anything on the basketball court without a purpose. If he went behind his back or made a no-look pass, it was because that was the way to get the job done."

There will always be debate about who is the best player ever. Some say Bill Russell or Wilt Chamberlain. Others would vote for Larry Bird or Kareem Abdul-Jabbar, Jerry West, Michael Jordan, or Oscar Robertson. Pat Riley, Johnson's former Laker coach and a close friend, makes no bones about his choice. "I spent ten years with the greatest player ever," said Riley. "Earvin was more than a great player, he was a coach on the floor. He has the heart of a great warrior. He simply would not be beaten. Even in practice, he'd find some way to win, whether it was a game of H-O-R-S-E or whatever. Who else could have been an all-star at five positions?"

When Magic announced his retirement, he left a void in the NBA that can never be filled. He in turn spoke movingly about the void he would feel without playing the game. "I'll miss the game. I'll miss the competition, the locker rooms, the sweat, the fellas," Johnson told *Sports Illustrated*. "I'll even miss the travel and the little injuries that seemed to become big injuries as I got older. But what I'll miss most is something that might seem trivial to most people: the uniform.

"That sounds silly, I know. But it was always

the uniform that made me feel special—in high school, in college and the pros. That's why I never sat on the bench in street clothes for games in which I couldn't play because of an injury. When I walked into the locker room on my first day as a Laker and saw my gold uniform hanging there, I cried. Off the floor I've always been Earvin. But in uniform, I was Magic."

Indeed, Magic made his first appearance on the Forum floor less than two weeks after he retired when he showed up to cheer his former teammates on. He was greeted by a standing ovation that lasted close to five minutes. Then Johnson watched the game, dressed in street clothes and sitting on the bench, where he encouraged and coached his former teammates. He had given up his uniform for good and while he missed wearing it, all of basketball will miss seeing him wear it as well, because Magic in uniform had come to represent all that was good about the game.

"This is a man who didn't just touch America, he touched the whole world," said young Knicks guard Mark Jackson, who was another of Johnson's friends. "Magic is basketball. He is what a lot of us are about."

7

Superstar Off the Court

Millionaire athletes are hardly a novelty anymore. Major-league baseball players' salaries average more than $800,000, and the average salary in the National Basketball Association is approaching $1 million a year. However, few players have significantly built on that wealth to become major figures in the business world. Indeed, many squander their dollars. Though players in recent years have become a bit more sophisticated about the way they handle their finances, the stories of athletes blowing fortunes on bad investments or excesses continue to proliferate. Athletes making huge salaries remain vulnerable to losing much of what they earn.

Again Magic Johnson is different. Just as he set new standards on the court, Johnson has been a trailblazer among athletes in the world of business. When he announced his retirement, his estimated worth was at least $50 million. He numbers among his friends not just Larry Bird and Isiah Thomas but moguls like Michael Ovitz, one of the most powerful dealmakers in Hollywood, and Joe Smith, president of Capitol Records, one of the recording industry's giants. Los Angeles business leaders have flocked to his benefits and dream camps for years, and Johnson in turn has sought out corporate bosses for advice and ideas. At the same time, Johnson has been a giant in the charitable community who has given of his own money and time to raise millions for a long list of worthy causes. In both business and charity, Johnson doesn't simply lend his name and money. He gets closely involved with all details. He's a hands-on boss of his many business enterprises. He oversees all aspects of his charitable endeavors, such as the annual all-star game and banquet he stages for the United Negro College Fund.

Johnson's fascination with the world of business isn't a recent development since he started making big money. He appreciated the business world as a child and dreamed of being a success away from basketball. Just as he was obsessed as a youngster by basketball, he was also fascinated by work. When in elementary school, he worked for his father's hauling business. Young Earvin, Jr., also created his own business by cutting lawns and doing other errands for neighbors. He had a series of jobs while still in Lansing. He worked for a time as a janitor. He helped work a soft-drink delivery route. He sometimes had two or three different jobs going, all fit in between school and basketball. Indeed, Johnson usually had his basketball with him when he reported to work at one of his various jobs. Whether walking or riding his bike, he dribbled his way to work. Although he had his basketball idols, Julius Erving being the biggest, he also idolized those men in the neighborhood who were successful in business.

In a 1990 *Sports Illustrated* interview, Johnson told of his fascination with local businessmen. "Back home in Lansing, there were two successful businessmen, Joel Ferguson and Gregory Eaton. Everybody admired them. They had nice houses, drove nice cars. They owned office buildings and had whole staffs of people. They were our heroes." Earvin eventually got a job as a janitor in one of the buildings owned by Ferguson, and he related that when working Friday nights cleaning offices, he would also dream. "I'd sit back in one of those big chairs and put my feet on the desk. I'd start giving orders to my staff. 'Do this, do that.' I'm a big dreamer. And for some reason, I'd still like to own an office building."

Early on in his career, Johnson became determined to be a role model for young blacks, beyond just basketball. He said in a *Sports Illustrated* interview, "I was given the gifts to become not only an athlete but also a businessman, a thinker who could help dispel the myth that most athletes are dumb jocks who can't see beyond the next game. I'm glad that I have earned about $12 million annually in endorsement income in recent years but I'm happier about the fact that my business success has helped so many young blacks to learn that they can become entrepreneurs, and if they play ball, they can be both athletes and businessmen."

Johnson learned his work ethic from his father, Earvin, Sr., who worked two jobs to support the family of twelve and who made sure his son worked and worked hard. "All the things he taught me paid for me," said Johnson. "I see everything he was trying to teach me. I look for nothing from nobody. I have always worked for whatever I wanted. He stressed the importance of school to us because he never got a chance to go himself. He used to tell me 'I don't want to see you end up in this factory like I did.' "

In time, Johnson could end up owning the factory instead. Johnson has lucrative endorsement contracts with a number of major firms such as Pepsi, Kentucky Fried Chicken, Converse basketball shoes, Spalding, Nintendo, Target Stores, and CBS-Fox Video. In addition, Johnson has become an international commodity. He has a commercial association with a Spanish meat-packaging company named Campofrio. The company paid him more than $1 million to come to Spain for appearances and some youth basketball clinics. Johnson, like other NBA stars including Michael Jordan, is very conscious of the potential in the foreign market since NBA basketball has had growing international exposure. Participation in the Olympics would only add to the worth of the foreign market.

Johnson's future endorsement power according to some sports marketing people could be hampered by his sudden retirement due to the HIV virus. Some believe the admission that he is HIV-positive could cost him commercial associations because Johnson's new image is related to a disease which has a stigma that eventually will turn off the advertising community.

However, the other side of the equation according to some, reflects Johnson's display of courage openly acknowledging his infection, and his enthusiasm for being a spokesman has created a highly positive image among consumers. Analysts point out that companies are different in the 1990s. They want to make a difference in society and get involved in issues like the environment, education and, in Magic's case, the fight against AIDS. Brandon Steiner, a sports marketing consultant, said "Magic Johnson could break some serious ice. Companies may not be thinking about how fast they can get out of contracts with him but how they can get on his train. He can do commercials for Kentucky Fried Chicken, which could donate money from each meal to fight the virus and offer educational materials in their stores. If I were a company I'd call and see how I can get involved with him."

In the days immediately after Johnson's announcement, the companies with which he was associated told him that they wanted to continue their association. One, Spalding sporting goods, announced a plan to use Johnson in conjunction with an AIDS education message. Johnson moved cautiously in the days after his illness became public. "We're sifting through everything and Magic is going to be very, very selective to choose the most effective way to get out this message," said Lon Rosen, Johnson's business manager. "As for his commercial associations, everybody who is connected with him called and said they're standing behind him all the way. He's never had any fear or concern about that. That's why he chose companies like Pepsi, Spalding, Converse, Kentucky Fried Chicken, Target Stores—because he knew they were first-class."

Whatever happens with Johnson's commercial endorsements, they have become only part of his financial worth. Athletes like Bo Jackson, Michael Jordan, and Joe Montana approach or even surpass the total dollars Johnson makes from his endorsements. But none have put together as impressive a corporate portfolio as Johnson. And none have worked as hard to develop so many growing corporate enterprises.

Johnson founded a sports-apparel company that takes in close to $10 million a year. Magic Johnson T's is the fastest growing license holder in NBA history, expanding to the point at which it is among the top sellers of NBA apparel in the world. Johnson is expanding the company to manufacture NFL T-shirts and is interested in marketing major-league baseball and hockey shirts in the near future. Johnson didn't merely lend his name to something run by somebody else. He makes the final decisions on everything to do with the business, from finances to the design of the shirts.

In the summer of 1990, Johnson went a step further in the business world when he closed a major business deal with Pepsi by becoming general partner in a soft-drink distributorship in suburban Washington, D.C., that does close to $50 million in business a year. Johnson owns one-third of the distributorship after investing between $15 and $20 million. No active athlete has ever been involved in a business even close to the level of Johnson's deal with Pepsi. As with his T-shirt business, Johnson is more than just a name and a checkbook. Especially during the off-season, Johnson will travel to Washington for two or three days at a time, meeting with as many as possible of the 170 plant and adminis-trative personnel, meeting with key customers, selling the idea of putting Pepsi machines in businesses, and otherwise taking very seriously his role as a chief corporate officer of a major firm. Executives at the plant were pleasantly surprised at Johnson's intention to be a hands-on owner. "He's called Earvin around here; actually he's called Mr. Johnson," said one of the distributorship's employees.

Johnson began another business called Magic Johnson All-Star Camps which operates basketball camps in the summer for kids. And it also runs camps for business executives, who pay $5,000 each to come to Hawaii and play basketball for a week with Magic. He in turn has made these sessions with the corporate basketball players into personal seminars during which he gets from the businessmen all kinds of financial advice. Finally, Johnson recently formed Magic Johnson Enterprises, which in 1991 opened his Magic 32 clothing store.

His ultimate dream is to someday own the Lakers, or failing that, a professional sports franchise. He has already had some talks about the subject with Lakers owner Dr. Jerry Buss, who has recently been rumored to be interested in selling in the coming years. In fact, at Johnson's retirement press conference, he mentioned that the media could someday still find him at the Forum, though it would be in the owners' office and not the locker room. "My goal is to be in that one-hundred-to-two-hundred-million-dollar range which is basically what you got to have to buy a franchise," he said. "I'd like it to be the

Lakers but it doesn't have to be them. It doesn't even have to be an NBA team. I'm a sports fan. If baseball became available before basketball, I'd be right there."

As active a businessman as Johnson has become, he has also been a dynamic worker for charitable endeavors since his rookie days. Many AIDS activists and researchers are excited by his proven track record for charitable involvement. He's a seasoned fund-raiser, so his vow to become an AIDS spokesman offers much hope that he can work at the forefront of efforts to turn around the battle against the disease. Certainly his commitments over the past several years have been staggering. He annually stages a celebrity golf tournament for the benefit of the American Heart Association that raises close to $200,000. He is active in the Boys Clubs of America. He hosts dinners for such organizations as the Muscular Dystrophy Association and the City of Hope, a national medical research center in California that works on incurable diseases. He personally has contributed more than $100,000 a year for several years to Rust College in Mississippi.

Johnson is an easy touch for charities wanting a piece of his memorabilia to auction off in fund-raisers. He donates used shoes or basketballs to countless organizations. He has also raised hundreds of thousands of dollars through one-on-one contests in which individuals pay a large fee to play against him, with the money going to the charitable sponsor.

Johnson's largest charitable association has been with the United Negro College Fund, an organization that raises money and distributes it to forty black schools around the country. Magic chose the UNCF when he decided he wanted to begin staging his own fund-raisers for a charity instead of merely lending his name and money to other people's efforts. He wanted to create his own fund-raising events and target them for a deserving cause. Johnson had his business advisers research several groups and eventually decided upon the UNCF.

Johnson's association with the UNCF has become a remarkable one. In the beginning, Johnson had worried about whether he could attract enough players to make an all-star game fundraiser attractive enough to be successful. But his first game was a sellout, with scalpers getting $100 a ticket. The game has grown into the NBA's premier off-season event, bringing together the biggest stars in the game. In conjunction with the game are at least two banquets. Johnson has now staged six "Midsummer Night's Magic" events to sold-out crowds at the Forum, raising close to $5 million in the process. Johnson stays on top of every detail for the banquet and the game, going over seating arrangements and cocktail party plans and arranging accommodations for players like Larry Bird, Michael Jordan, Charles Barkley, Isiah Thomas,

Patrick Ewing, and all the others who jump at Magic's invitation and fly to Los Angeles for the charity game. Vincent Bryson, the UNCF's Southern California development director, told *Sports Illustrated*, "Magic is a fund-raiser's dream. People's motivations for doing good work are sometimes suspect. People have all kinds of needs and sometimes expect the charity to meet those needs. But Magic has the most unselfish attitude I've ever seen. He is not interested in promoting himself."

For Johnson, however, the active charity work is second nature. "People have helped me all my life and it just seems natural that I should help others now," he said. "Ever since I was a kid, people have given their time to help me. First of all there was my dad and my coaches. But then there were people like Jim Dart, who gave his time to coach us when we didn't have any basketball program. There were people like Joel Ferguson and Gregory Eaton back home who taught me that even if I was growing up, struggling a little in Lansing, I could have my dreams and my ambitions.

"I can't understand other players who don't get involved in charities and in their communities. There are guys who won't speak or won't appear or ask how much will they get paid. Somebody helped them out once. I know somebody helped me out and I don't ever want to forget."

Johnson now faces his greatest business and

charitable challenge. He would seem well equipped to join the fight against AIDS. He has excellent business sense. He has widespread and powerful contacts among major businessmen and Hollywood stars, a combination that could be an excellent fund-raising tool on behalf of AIDS research. He is financially secure, which should allow him to devote as much time as necessary to fighting the disease. Most of those stricken don't have such a luxury. "My goal now is to help young people, especially young blacks, to understand AIDS," he said. "I look at this as an opportunity for which I am in the right position to help."

Indeed, within days of his retirement, Johnson had begun forming a foundation called "Project 32" to foster AIDS research and education.

8

Magic's Toughest Challenge

Ironically if not for a decision to renegotiate his contract with the Los Angeles Lakers, Magic Johnson might never have learned that he had contracted the HIV virus and would not have retired from basketball. Johnson might have gone on playing for months or years without getting tested for AIDS, at a cost to him and those around him that could have been many times more devastating.

However, in early September, Johnson and his agent Lon Rosen had opened talks with the Lakers. Under the terms of a contract signed several years previously, Johnson was to be paid $2.5

million in the 1991–92 season. It was a hefty sum to be sure, but still below the numbers of several other NBA players, including teammate Sam Perkins. Lakers owner Jerry Buss and general manager Jerry West both agreed with Johnson that he should receive a bigger salary that would better reflect his status and worth according to the current market conditions.

The National Basketball Association's salary cap system limits a team's total payroll. Since the Lakers were at their salary limit, they were prevented from giving Johnson a new contract or even an extension to the contract he had that ran through the 1993–94 season. However, the Lakers came up with the idea of giving Johnson more money through a low-interest loan, which was permissible under NBA rules. That plan was agreeable to Johnson, and the two sides settled on a $3 million payment, which Johnson received at the end of September.

As was routine in such big-dollar transactions, the Lakers then took out a new insurance policy on Johnson as protection against the $3 million loan. The insurance company asked that Johnson take a routine physical examination before the insurance policy was approved. It was then that things became anything but routine. The insurance company informed the Lakers that it had rejected the policy for unspecified medical reasons. Johnson, through the Lakers' team doctor, asked for an explanation. The explanation changed Magic's life forever.

Johnson was in a Utah hotel room resting for a Lakers exhibition game October 25 when Dr. Michael Mellman, one of the team's physicians, called and told him to fly immediately to Los Angeles to discuss the results of the insurance examination. Even then, Magic had no idea of the news that awaited him. He felt in excellent physical condition after rigorous workouts over several weeks in preparation for his thirteenth NBA season. He had played well in exhibition games. He had felt some fatigue in recent days, but he attributed that to the rigors of a trip with the Lakers to Paris, where he was the MVP of the McDonald's Open tournament. When Dr. Mellman urged his immediate return to Los Angeles, Johnson's first thought was that he might have high blood pressure, something his father had suffered from most of his life.

In Los Angeles, Dr. Mellman sat Johnson down and told him that he had tested positive for the HIV virus. Like most Americans, Johnson was not well informed concerning the virus. When Mellman told him the news, Johnson thought he had AIDS, when actually he had the virus that eventually leads to AIDS. Johnson thought he would soon die. He thought of his wife, Cookie. Cookie had been his college sweetheart and they'd married on September 14, 1991. He immediately feared that Cookie, who was now seven weeks pregnant, might also be infected.

Johnson immediately told Cookie the awful news. He told her that he would understand if she wanted to leave him and that he wouldn't stand in the way if she wanted a divorce. "Before I could get most of my words out of my mouth, she slapped me upside the head and said I was crazy," said Johnson on Arsenio Hall's show. "Cookie is a very strong woman. Marrying her is the smartest thing I've ever done."

Over the next several days, Johnson would learn much more about AIDS and the HIV virus. He first underwent a second series of tests to make sure the insurance company's diagnosis was correct. Advised not to practice with the Lakers, he continued to work out on his own while missing the season's first three games. He would have long sessions of practicing jump shots to keep sharp for a season he still thought he would play.

When Johnson's additional medical tests returned, the original diagnosis was confirmed. Johnson had tested HIV positive. Good news, however, was that the tests on Cookie were negative, which means that she and the baby are thus far, free from the HIV virus. "When I heard that, things got a little easier," Johnson told Arsenio Hall. "When I heard they were okay, I had something to live for." Johnson began educating himself on the virus, reading information provided by his doctors so he could better understand the disease and the challenges before him. He learned that he would likely have AIDS (which stands for Acquired Immune Deficiency Syndrome) within ten years. He also learned that with the proper medication and diet, he could lead a normal life until the disease began breaking down his immune system. He learned that an enormous amount of worldwide research was continuing. He learned that the research needed funding, and that the U.S. government didn't seem interested in increasing money spent on the disease.

The more he read and the more he realized that he might not feel the effects of the virus for years, Johnson continued to believe he would play for the Lakers. However, after the original diagnosis was confirmed, Johnson's doctors told him that the physical and emotional strain of playing the long NBA schedule could weaken his immune system. They advised him to retire immediately from professional basketball. As much as Magic loved the game, he calmly accepted their judgment because he realized he had greater challenges to face.

Magic's first courageous decision was to go public with the news. He had already missed the Lakers' first three games of the season and was not showing up for practice. His teammates and the media were becoming increasingly suspicious that something was wrong. The Lakers had been explaining Johnson's absence by saying he had the flu, but that explanation was beginning to be questioned. Whispers were beginning to circulate around the always gossipy NBA that Johnson was seriously ill. There was one widely circulated rumor that he had a heart condition.

Philadelphia 76ers star Charles Barkley said, "Some rumors were floating around a week before Magic retired, around when he first went out with the flu. But you know those kinds of rumors are usually unfounded. You always hope and pray they're not true."

There was more to Johnson's decision to go public than a desire to quiet the rumors. He had studied the statistics on AIDS. He learned that over 1 million Americans were HIV-positive, that 125,000 Americans had already died of AIDS, that half the AIDS sufferers in America were either black or Hispanic. Magic felt an obligation to the country, especially to the minority community, to try and make it more aware of this disease that was finding new victims all the time. Like most other Americans, Johnson had always believed that AIDS was a disease reserved for homosexuals and drug users, not for someone like himself who was heterosexual and was vocally antidrug. Now Johnson knew different, and he became determined to act as a spokesman in the fight against the HIV virus and a visible advocate for safe sex.

Johnson had the Lakers schedule a 3 P.M. (Pacific Time) press conference for Thursday, November 7. Before meeting the press, Johnson called five close friends—Larry Bird, Arsenio Hall, Isiah Thomas, Pat Riley, and Michael Jordan—and told them he was infected with the AIDS virus. Johnson reported in *Sports Illustrated* that Bird and Arsenio cried. Isiah refused to believe the news, while Riley and Jordan listened in stunned silence. Johnson also called his ten-year-old son Andre, who lived with his mother in Michigan. Before meeting with the press, Johnson met with his teammates. Johnson would later say that that locker-room meeting was the most emotional episode of the entire ordeal. When he broke the news, his teammates wept, and, according to Magic, for the only time so did he. Then, composing himself, he walked out to tell the world, via live TV and radio. The next night, Johnson went on Arsenio Hall's popular late-night talk show and repeated the poised, upbeat performance he had given at his press conference.

The immediate press reaction was overwhelmingly positive. From a *New York Times* editorial to radio and TV talk shows, columnists lamented the devastating loss to the sport while heaping praise on Johnson for the courage it took to come forth with the devastating news. There were also whispers in the background surrounding the question, How did Magic contract the virus? Rumors immediately sprang up suggesting that Johnson was gay or bisexual, that he had been seen frequenting gay bars around Los Angeles. On the Arsenio Hall show, Johnson dismissed the rumor-mongers. "I'm far from homosexual," he said. "You know that, everybody who's close to me understands that. People can say what they want. I don't care. I'm thick-skinned and if they don't believe me or want to talk trash, I don't care because I won't hear them."

In a later *Sports Illustrated* interview, Johnson elaborated on the question of how he acquired the virus. "I am certain that I was infected by having unprotected sex with a woman who has the virus," he said. "The problem is that I can't pinpoint the time, the place or the woman. It's a matter of numbers. Before I was married, I truly lived the bachelor's life. I was never at a loss for female companionship. I confess that after I arrived in L.A. in 1979, I did my best to accommodate as many women as I could—most of them through unprotected sex."

Johnson went on to say in the magazine interview, "I'm being a man about my past. I'm not running from anyone. As soon as the test results were confirmed, I started calling some of the women I used to date and telling them that I am HIV-positive. Some of them are scared but I'm hoping that all of them will get tested and that they will all be O.K.

"I'm sure most of America has heard rumors that I am gay. Well, you can forget that. Some people started the talk during the NBA Finals in 1988 and 1989 when I kissed Isiah on the cheek as a pregame salute to our friendship and our respect to the game. But actually, I've been hearing that kind of talk for a long time. The most widely known fact about AIDS in the U.S. is that it affects homosexuals and intravenous drug users more than anybody else. But that's changing faster than the rest of us would like to believe.

"I sympathize with anyone who has to battle AIDS, regardless of his or her sexual preference, but I have never had a homosexual encounter. Never. I know that won't satisfy some people but it really doesn't matter what they might say about me. From the jokes down on Wall Street to the Magic-must-be-gay stories that will still circulate, none of it matters. My skin is real thick and as long as those same people who are telling jokes and trading stories are getting tested and changing their lifestyles and practicing safe sex, I'll win anyway."

Johnson's frankness blunted the rumors. But after the first wave of praise, some columnists began to have second thoughts. Pulitzer Prize-winning columnist Dave Anderson of *The New York Times* wrote a November 14 column titled, "Sorry, but Magic Isn't a Hero." Anderson wrote, "He has been hailed by many as a hero when hedonist might be the better word. . . . If one definition of 'hero' is model or ideal as Webster's Third New International Dictionary attests, Magic Johnson is hardly a model or ideal to anyone with a sense of sexual morality. Magic's message now is 'If I can get it, anybody can.' But anybody with a sense of heterosexual responsibility isn't likely to get the HIV virus. . . . Magic Johnson is a victim, not a hero."

Robert Lipsyte in the November 15 *New York Times* wrote a column titled "Magic as Hero: It's

Not the Most Comfortable Fit." Lipsyte wrote
"There are already commentators who maintain
that Johnson brought down his own house, that
his invoking of 'God's way' is specious, that his
message of safe sex is immoral.

"Think about all the women that Johnson may
have infected. They will suffer with less support.
And think about the irony of how he discovered
he was infected. He took a blood test to get a
policy to insure a no-interest loan the Lakers
were giving him to circumvent the salary cap the
league places on each team."

Lipsyte intimated that Johnson and his han-
dlers had orchestrated a public relations blitz
that rivaled a political campaign. In fact, Johnson handled himself in his usual style of leadership and control.

George Will and conservative politicians like
Vice-President Dan Quayle suggested that Johnson's message should not be "safe sex" but
rather "abstinence." Like so much having to do
with the AIDS issue, conservatives wanted to
make it a political issue. They seemed unable or
unwilling to grasp the fact that those who are
most likely to be influenced by Johnson's message are young adults who have grown up living
in a promiscuous world, both in the minority
community and throughout society. They are
young people, millions of them, who are going to
have sex, even if Dan Quayle tells them to "just
say no." It seems realistic to believe that a safe-
sex message coming from a much-loved public

figure like Magic Johnson is far more likely to hit home with them than preaching abstinence. The bottom line is to stop the spread of AIDS, not to make a political point.

There were also cynics who pointed out that the stocks of companies producing condoms rose on the New York Stock Exchange and that a Magic Johnson condom would likely hit the market.

Some people were missing the point. Johnson never claimed to be a hero. Most people who called him a hero did so because of his honesty in being so upfront about why he was retiring from basketball. Others were inspired by Magic's upbeat determination to try and make a difference in the fight against AIDS. Johnson was frank about the promiscuity that could cause his death, and he didn't try to defend his former lifestyle. He promised to try and influence others against emulating him. As he said in *Sports Illustrated*, "I'm pleading for every athlete and entertainer who has also been "out there" to get tested and from now on to practice safe sex. It doesn't matter how beautiful the woman might be or how tempting she might sound on the telephone. I know that we are pursued by women so much that it is easy to be weak. Maybe by getting the virus, I'll make it easier for you guys to be strong."

No one is trying to make Johnson into a god. Magic seemed to be seeking strength in his greatest time of need and turned to the spiritual

backbone he had been given by his parents since
he was a child. Magic has dealt with this tragedy
by believing that, as he told *Sports Illustrated*
"It's God's way. He is now directing me to be
come a teacher, to carry the message about the
danger of AIDS to everyone. . . . In everything
I've done, he's directed me. This is just another
way." Who can argue with him? The inner peace
he exhibited at his press conference and on Ar
senio Hall's show seemed ample proof that
Magic had spiritual strength.

One reason Johnson has been praised for his
courage is that he has elected to confront head
on a disease which until now has mainly been
discussed in whispers. When actor Rock Hudson
died of the disease, his feelings were only re
vealed after his death. Other famous people sim
ilarily affected have hidden from the spotlight
instead of seeking it. Some suggest Johnson is
guilty of self-promotion because of his forthright
revelations.

What is there for Johnson to gain if it is self
promotion? Johnson, who is worth close to $100
million, certainly doesn't need money. Self-pro
motion isn't going to help him in his battle
against the disease. Johnson has gone public in
order to help fight a growing menace to society
He vows to lead a crusade, and there are thou
sands of youngsters who will listen and follow
his lead.

Johnson didn't take long to move quickly into
his new leadership role. He accepted a position

on the President's National Commission on AIDS. The appointment will provide Johnson with a highly visible forum from which to get his message to young people and at the same time urge the government and private sector to provide more financing for AIDS research and education.

Johnson also is setting up a foundation called Project 32, through which he intends to support AIDS research and education.

Magic Johnson has been a leader all his life on and off the basketball court. Who can doubt that Earvin Johnson will now be a leader in the biggest challenge he has ever undertaken?

9

Magic's New Role

It is a measure of the nation's misunderstanding of the HIV virus that when Magic Johnson first announced he had been infected, millions of fans immediately wept in the belief that he would soon die. However, Earvin Johnson remains very much with us. He remains an active, vital man even while beginning treatment to combat the virus that leads to the AIDS disease.

He was at a Lakers game less than two weeks after announcing he had the HIV virus. He is continuing to maintain his busy business schedule. He will become a member of the President's National Commission on AIDS. He vows to embark on a crusade to educate the masses on the AIDS virus and safe sex. He promises to speak out in Congress and at the White House while working with businesses to increase funding for AIDS research. He says he still might play for the U.S. Olympic team at Barcelona in 1992.

Johnson may still be healthy enough to go out on the basketball court and be Magic once again. In the days after his retirement, he frequently went out of the way to emphasize that he was alive and still kicking. In the process, he has begun the nation's education. He is showing what it means to be HIV-positive, and he has been reassuring. "No one has to run from me," he said. "When you see me, you can still ask me for autographs and high fives. I'm going to be the same guy I've always been. I'm not all of a sudden someone you should be afraid of being around." His friends, after recovering from the initial shock, also tried to emphasize that Johnson had not departed from the scene. Said his close friend Isiah Thomas of the Detroit Pistons, "He woke up this morning. The sun came out. He ate breakfast. He's going to have lunch, dinner. He's going to sleep again tonight." And said another friend, former Lakers coach Pat Riley, "We don't want to eulogize him. His career is over in basketball but his life still goes on."

It is conceivable that Johnson could remain healthy for years, for that is the insidious nature of the virus. No one knows how long Johnson has before his virus becomes full-blown AIDS. Many patients with the HIV virus live comfortably ten or twelve years, sometimes longer. The simple fact is that doctors don't know how quickly AIDS will appear and attack any individual infected with the HIV virus. Nor does Johnson's peak physical condition as a world-class athlete necessarily give him an edge in fighting the disease.

In the decade or so since AIDS was first named, researchers have made progress against it. They have identified its cause, the HIV virus which now infects Johnson as well as more than 1 million other Americans. Doctors have devised reliable tests that can determine the presence of the HIV virus, thus not only aiding early detection of the virus as in Johnson's case, but also minimizing the risk of contracting it through blood transfusions. Drugs have been discovered that slow the growth of the virus and delay the onset of AIDS. Other drugs treat many of the complications of AIDS. It has been reliably determined that if people follow certain rules, the spread of the virus can be halted. The one thing that hasn't been found is a cure. Once a person like Earvin Johnson or any one else contracts the HIV virus, he has it for life.

Johnson announced he would soon begin treatment. A couple of weeks after his press conference he began taking the drug AZT, which is the standard treatment for HIV. As he told *Sports Illustrated*, "I'm eager to begin the process that will help me someday to beat this thing." Indeed, all hope is not lost for Johnson and the millions of other sufferers. Medical science continues to work toward finding a way to transform AIDS into a treatable chronic disorder that would allow sufferers to lead normal lives and live to their normal length of years. What's needed is increased awareness to prevent further spreading of the disease, especially in minority communities, where it has been growing the fastest. Also needed is increased funding, both from the government, since the Bush administration has been reluctant to press for more spending, and from companies and private donations.

Earvin Johnson can make a huge impact. AIDS has never had a spokesman of Johnson's universal appeal. Some AIDS activists called Johnson's announcement the biggest thing to happen to AIDS since the AIDS-related death of actor Rock Hudson in 1985. However, the impact of Johnson's admission far exceeds the effect of the news about Hudson. Johnson's appeal dwarfs that of the aging actor. Johnson's popularity rivaled that of any celebrity superstar, whether Michael Jordan, Bo Jackson, Arnold Schwarzenegger, or Bruce Springsteen. Old and young, rich and poor, black and white, men and women, fans and non-fans were stunned by the news. The amazing outpouring of emotion indicated that Magic is indeed one of a special breed, a mythic presence of enormous talent who was made accessible by his tremendous personality and beautiful smile. Magic is simply seen as a nice guy. No one could dislike him.

He has been a sports idol who rivaled the all-time greats in popularity and appeal. He seemed to be largely immune from criticism. The admission that he had been infected with the AIDS virus certainly hurt his image in some quarters. Streetwise kids were heard to say things like "Magic was too smart to get messed up with AIDS." There were inevitable whispers about Magic's private life and the threat that the media will dig for whatever dirt it can find to fling at his image. However, the weeks immediately after Johnson's statement had very little of that sort of reaction. Instead, there was a genuine sadness and, more importantly, a significant increase in AIDS awareness.

Only time will tell how Johnson will fashion his new self-created role as a spokesman for the fight against the disease and for safe sex as a preventive measure. However, the response immediately after Johnson's November 7 retirement was illuminating. On the day of his announcement, the National AIDS Hotline received more than 40,000 calls. It usually averages close to 4,000. The Centers for Disease Control logged 10,000 AIDS-related calls in the first hour after Johnson's announcement. AIDS information centers and testing facilities reported unprecedented inquiries in the weeks after Johnson's admission, a flood that in many cases forced a wait of several weeks for testing because the understaffed and underfunded facilities simply could not keep up with the demand.

Johnson will certainly bring a huge presence to the AIDS fight. Not only is his image excellent and his popularity immense. He also has unique credibility. He is not just another celebrity lending his name to a charitable cause. He is one of the disease's victims, who also happens to be one of the most visible and popular individuals in the country.

But how much difference can he make? On that there will be debate, and indeed only time will tell. But there is reason to hope that he will have a significant impact. The openness with which he discussed his infection indicated how far the country had come in awareness in the years since Rock Hudson hid his illness until his dying days. Johnson's public discussion of his HIV infection, as he remains visibly healthy, has generated national sympathy and an apparent resolve to start doing something about AIDS. Johnson is indeed an easy leader to follow for corporations, for government, and for individuals. He is a much-loved superstar and does not conjure up less acceptable images of AIDS such as drug use and homosexuality.

As a black sports hero, Johnson will be better able to reach inner-city youths than virtually any other spokesman imaginable. Still, it has been proven through the years that just making people aware of a problem doesn't solve it. The fight against AIDS can hardly turn around overnight, not when at least 50,000 people are being infected with the HIV virus every year, when more than 1 million already have the virus, when 200,000 currently have developed full-blown AIDS, and when more than 125,000 have already died. An estimated 2,000 babies a year are born with the HIV virus. The threat of the disease's spreading through heterosexual contact had at first been largely dismissed. However, in recent years, that threat has begun to grow, as evidenced by Magic Johnson's insistence that he became infected through contact with a woman. On the one hand, the risk is lower through heterosexual contact. On the other hand, it exists and Johnson's safe-sex plea can be helpful to everyone.

AIDS has been a political and financial issue, and that is where Johnson's impact will be interesting as well. Though his presence on the President's Commission should give that group needed additional exposure, it also should be noted that the commission has made a series of recommendations for increased funding, accelerated educational programs, and improved follow-up procedures that have been repeatedly ignored by President Bush. In Congress, where increased spending is under fire in all areas, requests for badly needed increased funding in the AIDS area have gone nowhere. Since the HIV virus in recent years has spread much more widely in the poor and minority communities, the need for more funding is only heightened. Instead, the number of cases keeps growing faster than the funding is increasing.

Given Johnson's corporate and Hollywood connections, he may have better success tapping the private sector for increased contributions for research and for disseminating more information. It seems likely that Johnson will use many of his commercial associations as vehicles for getting out the AIDS message. At the least, it is certain that his involvement will ensure that unprecedented new attention is given to the disease in the coming years. Even President Bush, who has given little attention to the AIDS problem, was moved to acknowledge in the wake of Johnson's admission that perhaps he had done too little in the past. Johnson's impact is already being felt in the highest echelons of America.

However, the AIDS issue remains highly volatile, and Johnson will always run the risk of having his image damaged in the process. Some activists maintained that Johnson's emphatic denials of homosexual activity reinforced the stigma of this largely being a disease for gays. But most AIDS activists believe that Johnson's involvement can only help their cause. Michael Weinstein, president of the AIDS Healthcare Foundation, said, "The main thing that raises awareness of the HIV virus or AIDS is to know someone who has it. Now everybody in America knows someone with HIV."

Indeed, Johnson's unique personality should be the most effective weapon yet employed to increase awareness of AIDS and the HIV virus. Johnson has said so far that he will work on prevention of the disease. He has not expressed bitterness or tried to lay blame for his infection. Instead, he has been upbeat and positive about his chances to beat the disease. He has seemed almost to relish the challenge.

"God has directed me in everything I have done," Johnson told Arsenio Hall. "And I can't look at this infection as anything other than an opportunity to do something that might end up overshadowing basketball. It's not easy to accept, not when it could have been so easily avoided if I had worn condoms. And sure, I was convinced that I would never catch the AIDS virus but if it was going to happen to someone, I'm actually glad it happened to me. I think I'll be able to spread the message concerning AIDS better than almost anyone.

"I don't have any fear. If I die tomorrow, I've had the greatest life anybody could imagine. I've lived a life that no one could have imagined for me or anyone else. This is another challenge in that life. I intend to fight hard to beat this disease. And I'm going to win."

Indeed, the fight against AIDS now has on its side the most valuable winner in all of sports.

MAGIC'S CAREER STATS

COLLEGE

Season	Team	G	Min.	FGM	FGA	FG%	FTM	FTA	FT%	Reb.	Pts.	Avg.
1977-78	Michigan State	30	—	175	382	45.8	161	205	78.5	237	511	17.0
1978-79	Michigan State	32	1-59	173	370	46.8	202	240	84.2	234	548	17.1
Totals		62	—	348	752	46.3	363	445	81.6	471	1059	17.1

NBA REGULAR SEASON

Season	Team	G	Min.	FG	FGA	FG%	FT	FTA	FT%	Off. Reb.	Def. Reb.	Total Reb.	Ast.	PF	Stl.	BS	Pts.	Avg.
1979-80	LA Lakers	77	2795	503	949	53.0	374	462	81.0	166	430	596	563	218	187	41	1387	18.0
1980-81	LA Lakers	37	1371	312	587	53.2	171	225	76.0	101	219	320	317	100	127	27	798	21.6
1981-82	LA Lakers	78	2991	556	1036	53.7	329	433	76.0	252	499	751	743	223	208	34	1447	18.6
1982-83	LA Lakers	79	2907	511	933	54.8	304	380	80.0	214	469	683	829	200	176	47	1326	16.8
1983-84	LA Lakers	67	2567	441	780	56.5	290	358	81.0	99	392	491	875	169	150	49	1178	17.6
1984-85	LA Lakers	77	2781	504	899	56.1	391	464	84.3	90	386	476	968	155	113	25	1406	18.3
1985-86	LA Lakers	72	2578	483	918	52.6	378	434	87.1	85	341	426	907	133	113	16	1354	18.8
1986-87	LA Lakers	80	2904	683	1308	52.2	535	631	84.8	122	382	504	977	168	138	36	1909	23.9
1987-88	LA Lakers	72	2637	490	996	49.2	417	489	85.3	88	361	449	858	147	114	13	1408	19.6
1988-89	LA Lakers	77	2886	579	1137	50.9	513	563	91.1	111	496	607	988	172	138	22	1730	22.5
1989-90	LA Lakers	79	2937	546	1138	48.0	567	637	89.0	128	394	522	907	167	132	34	1765	22.3
1990-91	LA Lakers	79	2933	456	976	47.7	519	573	90.6	105	446	551	989	150	102	17	1531	19.4
Totals		874	32287	6074	11657	52.1	4788	5649	84.8	1561	4815	6376	9921	2002	1698	361	17239	19.7

Three-Point Field Goals (Pct): 1979-80: 7-31 (22.6); 1980-81: 3-17 (17.6); 1981-82: 6-29 (20.7); 1982-83: 0-21; 1983-84: 6-29 (20.7); 1984-85: 7-37 (18.9); 1985-86: 10-43 (23.3); 1986-87: 8-39 (20 5); 1987-88: 11-56 (19.6); 1988-89: 59-188 (31.4); 1989-90: 106-276 (38.4); 1990-91: 80-250 (32.0). Totals: 303-1016 (29.8).

NBA PLAYOFFS

Season Team	G	Min.	FG	FGA	FG%	FT	FTA	FT%	Off. Reb.	Def. Reb.	Total Reb.	Ast.	PF	Stl.	BS	Pts.	Avg.
1979-80 LA Lakers	16	658	103	199	51.8	85	106	80.2	52	116	168	151	47	49	6	293	18.3
1980-81 LA Lakers	3	127	19	49	38.8	13	20	65.0	8	33	41	21	14	8	3	51	17.0
1981-82 LA Lakers	14	562	83	157	52.9	77	93	82.8	54	104	158	130	50	40	3	243	17.4
1982-83 LA Lakers	15	643	100	206	48.5	68	81	84.0	51	77	128	192	49	34	12	268	17.9
1983-84 LA Lakers	21	837	151	274	55.1	80	100	80.0	26	113	139	284	71	42	20	382	18.2
1984-85 LA Lakers	19	687	116	226	51.3	100	118	84.7	19	115	134	289	48	32	4	333	17.5
1985-86 LA Lakers	14	541	110	205	53.7	82	107	76.6	21	79	100	211	43	27	1	302	21.6
1986-87 LA Lakers	18	666	146	271	53.9	98	118	83.1	28	111	139	219	37	31	7	392	21.8
1987-88 LA Lakers	24	965	169	329	51.4	132	155	85.2	32	98	130	303	61	34	4	477	19.9
1988-89 LA Lakers	14	518	85	174	48.9	78	86	90.7	15	68	83	165	30	27	3	258	16.4
1989-90 LA Lakers	9	376	76	155	49.0	70	79	88.6	12	45	57	115	28	11	1	227	25.2
1990-91 LA Lakers	19	823	118	268	44.0	157	178	88.2	23	131	154	240	43	23	0	414	21.8
Totals	186	7403	1276	2513	50.8	1040	1241	83.8	341	1090	1431	2320	521	358	64	3640	19.6

Three-Point Field Goals (Pct.): 1979–80: 2-8 (25.0); 1980–81: 0-0; 1981–82: 0-4; 1982–83: 0-11; 1983–84: 0-7; 1984–85: 1-7 (14.3); 1985–86: 0-11; 1986–87: 2-10 (20.0); 1987–88: 7-14 (50.0); 1988–89: 10-35 (28.6); 1989–90: 5-25 (20.0); 1990–91: 21-71 (29.6). Totals: 48-203 (23.6).

NBA ALL-STAR GAME

Year Site	Min.	FG	FGA	Pct.	FT	FTA	Pct.	Off. Reb.	Def. Rsb.	Tot. Reb.	Ast.	PF	Stl.	Blk.	Pts.
1980 Landover, Md.	24	5	8	62.5	2	2	100.0	2	0	2	4	3	3	2	12
1982 East Rutherford, N.J.	23	5	9	55.6	6	7	85.7	3	1	4	7	5	0	0	16
1983 LA Lakers	33	7	16	43.8	3	4	75.0	3	2	5	16	2	5	0	17
1984 Denver	37	6	13	46.2	2	2	100.0	4	5	9	22	3	3	2	15
1985 Indianapolis	31	7	14	50.0	7	8	87.5	2	3	5	15	2	1	0	21
1986 Dallas	28	1	3	33.3	4	4	100.0	0	4	4	15	4	1	0	6
1987 Seattle	34	4	10	40.0	1	2	50.0	1	6	7	13	2	4	0	9
1988 Chicago	39	4	15	26.7	9	9	100.0	1	5	6	19	2	2	2	17
1989 Houston	Did not play—Injured														
1990 Miami	25	9	15	60.0	0	0	—	1	5	6	4	1	0	1	22
1991 Charlotte	28	7	16	43.8	0	0	—	1	3	4	3	1	0	0	16
Totals	302	55	119	46.2	34	38	89.5	18	34	52	118	25	19	7	151

Three-Point Field Goals (Pct.): 1980: 0-1; 1982: 0-0; 1983: 0-2; 1984: 1-3 (33.3); 1985: 0-0; 1986: 0-1; 1987: 0-0; 1988: 0-1; 1989: 0-0; 1990: 4-6 (66.7); 1991: 2-5 (40.0). Totals: 7-18 (38.9).

NBA Most Valuable Player: 1987, '89, '90.
All-NBA First Team: 1983, '84, '85, '86, '87, '88, '89, '90, '91.
All-NBA Second Team: 1982.
All-Rookie Team: 1980.
Playoff MVP: 1980, '82, '87.
All-Star Game MVP: 1990.
Member of NBA Championship Team: 1980, '82, '85, '87, '88.

NBA's All-Time Assist Leader (Regular Season and Playoff)
Led NBA in Assists: 1983, '84, '86, '87.
Led NBA in Steals: 1981, '82.
Led NBA in Free Throw Percentage: 1989.
Named to The Sporting News All-American First Team: 1979.
NCAA Division I Tournament Most Outstanding Player: 1979.
Member of NCAA Division I Championship Team: 1979.

Practical Information About HIV/AIDS

The AIDS virus is not in the air. It is not on things. It is in blood, semen, and vaginal fluids. AIDS is Acquired Immune Deficiency Syndrome. HIV is Human Immunodeficiency Virus. Over 125,000 Americans have died of AIDS since 1981. At least another million are infected with the HIV virus that may lead to AIDS. HIV is what causes the disease AIDS. HIV is blood-borne and transmitted sexually or through intravenous drug use. The virus attacks a person's immune system, a complex system of blood cells and other disease-fighting cells, which defends the body against infection. HIV eventually destroys important blood cells in the immune system, leaving the body unable to fight off infection and illness.

The best way to cope with AIDS is to be informed. Here are some important facts to understand:

- One of the biggest myths is that HIV is easy to catch. That is wrong. A person cannot get AIDS by drinking from a glass that someone with AIDS used.

- People don't have to worry about getting AIDS from sitting next to someone with the disease or working and playing with someone who has the disease, or using the same bathroom, or sharing clothes or food.
- Males and females of all backgrounds, cultures, colors, and sexual orientations can get the disease, although it is difficult to catch.
- HIV can be transmitted only through blood, semen, vaginal fluids, and sometimes breast milk. That is, it is transmitted by having unsafe sex with someone who has the virus or sharing a needle with someone who has the virus. Although much about the disease remains a mystery, the way in which it is transmitted is not in question.
- You cannot tell by looking at someone whether or not that person is infected with the virus. Most people with HIV look perfectly healthy.
- It is not true that someone found to have the HIV virus immediately is stricken with AIDS and becomes critically ill.

HIV is a virus that causes the AIDS disease. People like Magic Johnson who test HIV-positive can live normal lives, loving and living for as long as ten years or more before beginning to develop the series of illnesses or cancers known together as AIDS. There are treatments that are designed to slow the virus's attack on the body's immune system.

In recent years, researchers have been making some progress in treatments that allow HIV-positive people to manage the condition so that it may not advance into AIDS. Researchers are hopeful that the disease can someday be a manageable chronic condition (perhaps similar to diabetes). Unfortunately, many people have been reluctant to talk about the disease and confront its consequences. It is hard to believe that the AIDS epidemic has been with us for ten years now. But other immunodeficiency diseases have existed for thousands of years.

With the proper precautions, children, teenagers, and adults can protect themselves against acquiring HIV.

- Not using drugs is one precaution. A person can get AIDS from shooting drugs and sharing needles. Don't shoot drugs.
- Using any drug, including alcohol, is dangerous for another reason. It lowers a person's inhibitions and clouds judgment. This can lead directly to risky behaviors, such as unsafe sex.
- A person can be exposed to HIV by having unsafe sexual contact with someone who has the virus. To protect against acquiring HIV, anyone who is having sex must be careful and use appropriate protection. A person can abstain from having a sexual relationship, which is the best precaution. Many people postpone sex. Having a sexual relationship is an important personal choice that must be considered carefully.
- If people decide to have sex, any kind of sex, they should use condoms. You cannot tell who does and who doesn't have the virus. And many people who are infected don't know themselves that they have HIV. Safer sex means *always* using a condom so as not to take any risks.

If a person thinks he or she may have shared blood or semen with an HIV-positive person, the HIV-antibody screening test can indicate whether that person's body is responding to HIV infection by producing cells called antibodies, which at first fight the virus. Local AIDS information centers or hotlines provide information about where such tests and appropriate counseling are available. It takes up to six months for the antibodies to appear, so even if you have already been tested once, it is best to be retested *at least six months after* the last time you may have been infected through unsafe behavior. While no test is 100 percent accurate, this test shows false results less than 1 percent of the time. Counseling services are available before and after you take the test and receive the results.

Symptoms of HIV infection can be similar to those of other common infections. They include unexplained fever, chills, night sweats, white patches in the mouth (thrush), diarrhea, weight loss, persistent swollen glands or an unusual bump, swelling, skin rash, or lesion. You need not panic if you experience any of these symptoms, as they can represent many different treatable infections. However, if you believe you are at risk for HIV infection based on your sexual or drug-using activities, you should consult with a medical professional and discuss the possibility of testing.

There are agencies in every major city that supply AIDS information and services. Young people with questions should talk to their parents or teachers. Brochures and other educational materials are available through local community-health organizations. Books are available in schools, libraries, and bookstores. There are answers to many frequently asked questions and there are things you can do to keep yourself healthy.

Where do you go for help?

National AIDS Clearinghouse
NAC provides information and materials on HIV/
AIDS.
800-458-5231 or 800-243-7012

National AIDS Hotline
A 24-hour, toll-free service that provides confidential information about HIV/AIDS.
800-342-AIDS or 800-243-7889

Gay Men's Health Crisis
Provides newsletters about treatment for HIV/
AIDS.
212-807-6655 or 212-337-1950

Project Inform
Provides information about treatment for HIV/
AIDS.
800-822-7422

ABOUT THE AUTHOR

PETER PASCARELLI has been writing about sports for nearly twenty years for newspapers including *The National Sports Daily*, *The Philadelphia Inquirer*, *The Baltimore News-American*, and Gannett Newspapers. His work has also appeared in numerous other publications including *Esquire* and *The Sporting News*. A lifelong Boston Celtics fan, he nevertheless numbers Magic Johnson among his favorite all-time players.

We Deliver!
And So Do These Bestsellers.